Texts in
Computing Science

Volume 6

Automata
and
Dictionaries

Texts in Computer Science Series Editor
Ian Mackie

ian.mackie@kcl.ac.uk

Automata
and
Dictionaries

Denis Maurel
Université François-Rabelais de Tours
Laboratoire d'informatique

and
Franz Guenthner
Universität München
Centrum für Informations- und Sprachverarbeitung (CIS)

ISBN 1-904987-32-X
College Publications
Scientific Director: Dov Gabbay
Managing Director: Jane Spurr
Department of Computer Science
Strand, London WC2R 2LS, UK

Cover design by Richard Fraser, www.avalonarts.co.uk
Printed by Lightning Source, Milton Keynes, UK

Automata and Dictionaries

*How to represent a dictionary
for natural language processing*

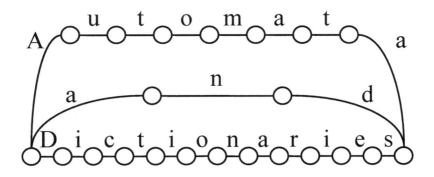

Examples and algorithms

We dedicate this book
to the memory of
Maurice Gross
(1934-2001)

One of the pioneers
in the use of finite-state technology
in many areas of
language processing

Preface

The automatic analysis of natural languages is of interest to all who deal with words and text in one manner or another, whether it is in the context of language learning, literary studies, linguistic analysis, historical studies, e-commerce or marketing, and many other interesting areas of scientific and practical work.

The topics we will address in this book seem to be very restricted at first sight and seemingly concern only computationally interested researchers in several related disciplines. Our main goal however is to reach as many interested readers as possible from a large variety of interest areas and for that reason we have tried to be as detailed and as clear as possible in every part of the presentation. We hope that at least from this point of view we have been successful.

More specifically this book is intended for:

- Scientists working in one area or another of natural language processing (also referred to as "computational linguistics"), whether or not they come more from a computer science or linguistics background.

- Undergraduate and graduate students in natural language processing or linguistics programs.

- Computer scientists and linguists interested in matters of language in one way or other.

- Computer scientists involved in teaching in any number of applied disciplines where there is always a need for ideas for algorithmic (and yet empirically motivated) exercises. In fact, the techniques used to represent and implement very large data sets (like dictionaries) can be of use in many other sectors where fast access to data (represented essentially in the form of lists) is of interest.

Chapter 1 tries to underscore the usefulness of large linguistic resources in language analysis, a topic that seems to us to have been very sadly neglected, especially during the last decade, where the emphasis on statistical methods for discovery and description has been overwhelming but where – in our opinion – interesting success stories as far as sophisticated applications are concerned are still very much outstanding. As we try to point out in the chapter, it is one thing to apply statistical algorithms on textual data, but it is quite another thing to select the "right entities" to which to apply them. As far as we know, there has not been any substantial progress in creating either sophisticated linguistic databases (e.g. monolingual or bilingual lexica, or parsers, or translation systems, etc.) on the basis of statistical approaches starting more or less from scratch as far as the enumeration of elementary linguistic facts are concerned.

The next chapter is a very elementary introduction to the subject matter of this book and presents the basic notions with a few very simple and naïve examples.

This chapter is followed by a more abstract presentation of the mathematical notions necessary to manipulate the objects and structures used to represent and implement dictionaries, namely, finite-state automata and finite-state transducers.

Readers not familiar with the basic mathematical concepts can skip over this chapter during the first reading. The next two chapters explain the fundamental concepts of determinization and minimization. We then move on in the next three chapters to the central material of this book, the construction of automata and transducers from (large finite) list of words.

Needless to say, there are quite a few interesting and related topics that we either do not mention at all or that are touched upon only marginally. This book has a rather narrow scope by design. Readers interested either in the history of the theory of automata might want to consult the synthetic overview in [Perrin, 1995]. Another very useful overview of finite-state techniques in natural language processing both from a linguistic and computational point of view is given in the papers brought together in [Roche, Schabes, 1997].

Contents

Contents

1. Automata, Dictionaries and Natural Language Processing

1.1 The role of dictionaries in natural language processing

1.1.1 A surprising observation

One of the most striking facts concerning the current state of scientific knowledge about languages is that for no existing natural language have we come anywhere close to constructing complete and systematic dictionaries of the basic linguistic building blocks that could be put to immediate use in a large variety of applications (such as automatic translation, information retrieval, grammar checking, etc.) and many other areas.

The problem is not only that we lack more or less complete lists of the "words" of a given language, together with their morphosyntactic codes; it is also highly likely that even in the case where at least partial lists of words with such information have been constructed, this information is both to a large extent too gross (if not to say erroneous) as well as seriously incomplete. Too gross, because the morphosyntactic "categories" assigned to most words do not really capture the morphosyntactic behavior of the words in an adequate way; nor are the necessary semantic characterizations of the words taken sufficiently into account. The point is that the now century-old categories "parts-of-speech" like "verb", "adjective", "noun", etc. used to characterize the morphological and syntactic properties of words are descriptively more than inadequate as they stand; they do not correspond in any reliable way to the way the words that they are used to classify actually show up and behave in real discourse. To limit oneself to saying for instance that "hatred" and "war" are both "nouns" in English does not really provide any kind of useful information apart from the fact that we accord them quasi-similar behavior with respect to other words categorized as "noun" as well; but what do words like "hatred", "war", "chair", "dog" or many thousand others really have in common: essentially nothing of course (apart from the fact that they co-occur often with some determiners). The situation is even worse with respect to "closed-word-class" (or grammatical) items for which there seems to no agreement even for the linguistic category terminology used to describe them. Words like "other", "some", "very" are described very differently (and put in the same buckets as other presumably similar words) in every attempt to list and describe them. As we shall see below there are still further deficiencies in existing "electronic dictionaries" that need to be overcome on the way to make them theoretically and practically useful.

This rather critical appraisal of the state-of-the-art of electronically available dictionaries does not preclude that today's and tomorrow's dictionaries need to be represented and implemented in a way that allows their use in electronic form to process text in a robust and efficient way. Even if the form and content of currently available electronic versions still leave a lot to be desired, the way that they can be computationally deployed in concrete applications has been extensively studied during recent years and deserves to be discussed and presented in a text book such as this one. Before we come to the main subject matter of this monograph, implementing dictionaries as finite-state devices (or automata), we would briefly like to go through a number of issues that will need to be considered on the way to more empirically adequate dictionaries in the future.

1.1.2 Dictionaries and lexical units

When talking about the design and implementation of (electronic) dictionaries we need to keep in mind a fundamental distinction between "words" in whatever disguise and "lexical units". As we will see below by far the great majority of interesting "lexical units" in any language are "multi-word" items as opposed to "simple-word" item. In this book, we also use the term *monolexical unit* for a word written with a sequence of letters and *polylexical unit* for a word written with at most one non-letter character. These polylexical units need to be classified in the same way as their monolexical unit counterparts. This is especially true for those polylexical units that have their own specific morphological, syntactic and semantic properties that cannot be predicted from any one of their parts.

One reason why for instance many purely statistical approaches to language analysis are not particularly successful is certainly to be found in the simple fact that the units of analysis (i.e. of counting and comparing) are in no way the "interesting" elements. There is also yet no evidence that all polylexical units can be discovered and then verified with statistical techniques alone; and without such units most statistical investigations will simply address spurious entities (e.g. the individual word forms) most of the time.

Lexical units can be found in a large variety of complex constructions in addition to the major syntactic categories like nouns, verbs, adjectives, etc. Of course, there are many polylexical nouns, adjectives or adverbs whose morphological forms do not admit much (internal) variation, but by far the large majority of polylexical units are to be found in the area of "fixed verbal predicates" and elementary sentence patterns that also need to be considered as lexical units in their own right. Below we will give a few examples of typical polylexical units. All of these can (and should) be represented and implemented as automata and transducers in our view. Electronic dictionaries constructed in the DELA fashion[1] typically make a distinction between four kinds of lexical databases: dictionaries for so-called "simple words" (monolexical units), for "compound words" (polylexical units), for fixed expressions and for "regular" predicative constructions. We discuss these in turn in the next sections.

1.1.3 Monolexical units

It seems at first that it should be a relatively easy matter to determine the set of monolexical units in a language. But this is not altogether a trivial enterprise. One reason is that we cannot simply assume that all sequences of letters occurring between some fixed

---

[1] Cf. below for more information on the dictionary work begun in the late 1980's at the LADL (*Laboratoire d'automatique documentaire et linguistique*) at the University Paris 7 under the direction of Maurice Gross and since extended to almost twenty languages at research centers around the world. (DELA stands for *Dictionaire électronique du LADL*.)

set of *separators* (e.g. spaces, punctuation signs, etc.) can be taken to make up the set of simple words (even in languages that have an orthographic tradition where such separators play a central role in the way we view the construction of lexical items[2]. Even for languages like German, Norwegian or Dutch, for instance, the assumption that orthographically separated words make up the set of monolexical units leads to enormous difficulties (see section 1.1.4, page 21).

In languages like English or French where blankless word compounding is not as pronounced as it is in other languages, it is often assumed that the use of separators determines at least the set of elementary forms that need to be inventoried in an exhaustive manner. And this has in fact been done for such languages in a variety of projects during the last 15 years. There are by now relatively large-scale databases of the monolexical units and their inflectional and derivational variants for dozens of languages. These dictionaries list practically all observed elementary or simple forms together with the relevant information about their flectional paradigms. The basic form of such dictionaries is always the same and contains, for the moment, the following types of information[3]:

<Full form, Lemma, Syntactic category, Morphological codes>

---

[2] As opposed to say languages like Chinese or Japanese where the notion of a separator is not given in the orthographic conventions of the language.

[3] The semantic classes for noun entries and construction codes for verbal entries in question are included in some version of DELA dictionaries; we have not specified these in the examples here.

Examples[4]:

- English: <dances,dance.V:P3>
  <dances, dance.N:p>

- French: <danses,danser.V:P2s:S2s>
  <danses,danse.N:fp>

- German: <tanze,tanzen.V:1eGc:1eGi:3eGc>
  <tanze,tanz.N:0:deM>

Such triples consist of the full-form as observed in text, the corresponding lemma form, a morpho-syntactic code containing an indication of the syntactic category (e.g. *V* for *verb* or *N* for *noun*) and an indication of the morphological features associated with the full form (e.g. singular, plural, tense, etc.).

Here is a short sample monolexical forms drawn from the appendix of this book:

```
place,.N:s
place,.V:W:P1s:P2s:P1p:P2p:P3p
planet,.N:s
planktonic,.A
plaque,.N:s
plate,.N:s
plate,.V:W:P1s:P2s:P1p:P2p:P3p
```

---

[4] There exist many formats for denoting the various syntactic and morphological features; for detailed descriptions one should consult the documentation by the authors of the dictionaries.

```
plates,plate.N:p
plates,plate.V:P3s
play,.N:s
play,.V:W:P1s:P2s:P1p:P2p:P3p
pneumonia,.N:s
point,.N:s
point,.V:W:P1s:P2s:P1p:P2p:P3p
polymerase,.N:s
polymeric,.A
polystyrene,.N:s
possibility,.N:s
possible,.A
```

Note however that these samples (and the dictionaries that were used to look them up) only indicate the morphosyntactic properties of the lemmas in question.

Among the many interesting research problem in connection with the inventory of monolexical units, we should mention the treatment of word forms which never or rarely occur alone but only in combination with other words forms such as *electro* as in *electro-chemical*, a problem which occurs frequently with hyphenated words, for instance.

1.1.4 Polylexical units

Among the many astonishing lacunae in current natural language processing research (and even more so in current applications as well) is the more or less complete absence of the notion of a dictionary of polylexical units, in particular of dictionaries of polylexical nouns[5]; this is equally true for languages like German where compounds are relatively easy to detect compared for instance to languages like English. Two things above all are of importance in connection with such dictionaries of polylexical units. The first is that – as previous research has amply shown[6] – the majority of lexical items in any language consists of polylexical nominal expressions like for instance "suffix tree", "board of directors", etc. [Gross, Senellart, 1998]. The second observation is that these polylexical nouns need to be coded in *exactly the same way* as monolexical nouns in terms of the morphological, syntactic and semantic properties. Little research on both the systematic way of constructing such dictionaries and on ways to encode them in a coherent and efficient way has been carried out. A notable exception is the work by Agata Savary [2000, 2005].

---

[5] The only notable exception are the research teams working in the tradition of the LADL, where great importance has been attached to the construction of such dictionaries since the late 1980s and where relatively sizable dictionaries of compound words have been made available for English, French, German, Portuguese and a few other languages. An interesting reference is the paper by Maurice Gross [1986]. A notable reference on why dictionaries of compounds are of interest for English is [Halpern, 2000].

[6] For instance, hand-curated dictionaries of polylexical nouns for German and English have reached several million entries on the basis of on-going work over fifteen years; for English, more than twenty million (!) candidates for polylexical words have been extracted from various large corpora including for instance the Web. We are currently in the process of extracting and encoding all frequent English compounds from a fifteen billion word corpus of English constructed over several years.

The reason why especially the dictionaries of polylexical nouns are of relevance in the present context is that very efficient and compact ways of implementing them are required, given their large size, to make full and effective use of them in concrete applications. Many experiments recently carried out at our institutes have shown that approximately 20–30% of running text is made up of such polylexical units. Even it were possible to identify them at run-time (which is far from being the case), there would be no point in recomputing them every time). And even if that were possible at least to some extent, all the information concerning the semantic and domain information including in a dictionary of such form would simply not be available at run-time.

1.1.5 Fixed (or frozen) phrasal expressions

The category of nominal expressions is of course not the only category that contains complex expressions, i.e. polylexical units made up from monolexical ones[7]. This is true for all syntactic categories of all natural languages; in general there are orders of magnitude more polylexical units than monolexical ones for every syntactic category that needs to be inventoried. Let us mention just a few in this connection.

Perhaps the most obvious candidates for where to look for large varieties of polylexical units are adverbial phrases and complex verbs. For instance, for German and French many thousands of

[7] For a recent survey of the various kinds of polylexical expressions, cf. [Guenthner, Blanco, 2004].

"idiomatic" adverbs have been coded[8]. There is simply no other way than to enumerate these lexical items and their syntactic variation and their semantic meaning than by enumerating them in a dictionary. How else could one deal with expressions like *John kicked the bucket* that will be translated as *John died* or by another idiomatic expression, like *John a cassé sa pipe*[9] in French or *John beisst ins Gras*[10] in German? Needless to say, it is pointless to try and deal with them via some form of syntactic combinatorial constraints or to translate such expressions on the basis of some (albeit arbitrary) translation of the words they contain.

In addition to the many thousand frozen polylexical adverbials (most likely somewhere around ten to twenty thousand for languages like English, German or French) there are even more frozen predicates that also need to be inventoried in a systematic way; here it is important to distinguish between "real" frozen predicates of the *John kicked the bucket* ilk and the many varieties of support verb constructions which need to be dealt with in an entirely different way. For instance, the meaning of the sentence *The surgeon operates on John for cancer of the throat* can also be expressed by *The surgeon carries out an operation on John for cancer of the throat*, where *to carry out* is a specific support verb combined with the predicative noun *operation*. Traditional (mainly

---

[8] Cf., for instance, [Gross, 1990] for French and [Engelke, 2003] for German.

[9] Translated word for word as *John broke his pipe*.

[10] Translated word for word as *John bites (into) the grass*.

printed) collections of such frozen predicates hardly exceed a few thousand entries; but recent research sets the number that should be formalized (together with their morphological and syntactic and semantic properties) much higher. It is to a large extent still an open research problem to what extent and how the kinds of (transducer) formalisms discussed below will be fully adequate to deal with them.

There are, in addition to the categories mentioned above, many frozen expressions in all other syntactic categories as well; this is true for connectives, complex determiners, interjections, etc. In fact, in addition to monolexical determiners like "every", "the", etc. there are thousands of polylexical ones, whose morphological and syntactic shape and whose meaning can in no way be predicted form their parts.

We should mention here that there are polylexical units of a kind that rarely seems to be noticed in the linguistic literature (Maurice Gross' approach to the classification of French verbs is perhaps the only real exception): namely the combinations of predicate expressions (whether they be of the verbal, nominal, adjectival or prepositional type) and the arguments they are – in some so far not completely understood manner – connected to. Regarded as complex lexical units, which they certainly should be, they are not however as one might expect the most numerous type of predications, but they also have not been specified extensively for any natural language so far. Ongoing research projects have however already shown the great merit of such enumerations[11]. An inkling of what kind applications, for instance in the area of machine translation, would then become possible can be gathered in a paper by Morris Salkoff on how information concerning the predicate-argument structure of elementary sentences can be put to effective use [Salkoff, 1992].

1.1.6 How many lexical items are there in a given natural language?

The brief survey of the many forms lexical units can take in natural languages gives rise to the question of how many lexical units we need to reckon with when we attempt to construct linguistically and computationally adequate electronic dictionaries. As far as we know, such questions have never been seriously addressed in the linguistic literature that we are aware of[12]. Of course, numbers concerning the inflected and base forms of monolexical units have been forthcoming; but even in the case of very complete systematic morphological dictionaries[13], the numbers are not as reliable as

---

[11] For instance, the lexical databases of frozen verbal expressions (around 30000) or of predicative noun construction (around 20000) constructed over the years at the LADL.

[12] Cf. [Guenthner, 2002] for some comments about how to count lexical items.

[13] For instance, for the French, English or German morphological dictionaries, which have been extensively tested on enormous amounts of data on a daily basis and which now have a recall of 99.5 on non-technical text.

they should be. The reason is not so much to be found in the pure coverage or recall aspect; it is rather the notion of what the real lexical items should be taken to be. Ambiguity of the entries is just one issue; the more important one is, as pointed out above, the recall with respect to the *intended lexical units*. Since the majority of the latter are indeed complex, measuring recall (or any other measure like for instance tagging correctness, etc.) with respect to their parts is not really significant.

Assuming that most simple forms are to count as bona fide lexical units somewhere, we have at least a lower bound on the lexical units.

This lower bound is typically around one to two million full-forms for languages like English and French if we omit very specific technical vocabulary[14]. It is more difficult to give precise numbers for languages that have different orthographic conventions for compound words as in the case of German, Dutch or Norwegian. At least some evidence is available from corpus studies already carried out. Let us take an example: a year's worth of comparable English or French newspaper text compared to a similar year's worth of German text will typically differ by a factor of five or more in the size of the monolexical word types due the orthographic conventions concerning compound units.

---

[14] If we include the latter, a much larger number of elementary lexical forms would have to be taken into account.

Depending on the size of the underlying corpus there are many reasons to believe that just the nominal vocabulary alone of languages with ongoing cultural and scientific communication will easily approach the ten million counts, again if we leave non-technical corpora aside. Of course, it would be silly to assume that such a vocabulary should be related to the active vocabulary, not to mention the intersection of the active vocabulary of typical speakers (another issue is how this relates to the union of the active vocabulary of all the speakers in a language community). Nothing could be further from the truth, but that is of course not the question that is really at issue here. We are not designing the electronic dictionaries we have in mind to mirror what typical speakers master actively or passively, but rather what the English-speaking community has produced as a whole as its working vocabulary. This is so much the more reasonable as we want to be able to cater for any application area whatsoever with a minimal amount of application-specific modification concerning these dictionaries in the order in which they may arise[15].

If we combine the above observations with what we said about complex lexical units in all the other syntactic categories, any reasonable electronic dictionary should easily be many magnitudes greater than what is currently available anywhere.

---

[15] Another study we recently carried out on a year's worth of the *Financial Times* revealed that the number of words occurring in every daily issue in that corpus amounted to approximatively ten to twenty thousand items depending on the choice of word normalization.

1.1.7 No grammars without dictionaries

A long time ago, Maurice Gross coined the notion of "lexicon-grammars", which he intended to be the symbiosis of observations stemming from lexicographical *and* grammatical investigations. He was originally mainly concerned with the study of (full-)verbs, but came very quickly to describing compound phrases, "idioms" and even sub-languages (e.g. the language of the stock market) in the same way. The major insight of his work really made clear that the properties of a given lexical item could only be studied adequately in the syntactic contexts (more specifically, the elementary sentence) in which the particular items occurred. As one might have expected, lexicographical descriptions are mainly seen to be a prerequisite for descriptions about the distributional, transformational and frozen forms of appearance of these very same items.

What Maurice Gross made crystal clear in much of his work was the fact that many of the properties we would typically consider relatively "free" variations amenable to syntactic rules are already forthcoming in the lexical descriptions of these items.

Adequate grammars must therefore be based on extensive lexicographical bases.

1.1.8 No applications without grammars

Let us now turn very briefly to what must be the "gold standard" of evaluation of any approach to the matters mentioned above, namely what purposes we might want to use them for. There are unfortunately no success stories to tell about useful applications of dictionaries and grammars beyond, say, spell-checkers[16]. There is no adequate "stylistic" or "grammar" checker in sight, there are no machine translation systems that come even halfway close to avoiding very humerous effects, and there is no information extraction system that can extract anything interesting beyond simple argument entities like proper names or similarly obvious constructions (and even these applications are far from being more or less satisfactory).

The reason is simply that we need more than just recognition of known (or partially known) elements. The main problem in (computational) linguistic analysis in addition to enumerating the basic lexical constructions is to account for the many types of *variation* (or *paraphrase*) forms in which these lexical constructions occur in real situations (or corpora).

There is no hope whatsoever of course – at least given today's computing potentials – to mirror all the variations in the form of a dictionary-like list of constructions (although this is not to be excluded from a logical point of view, given the right assumptions of how variation can in fact arise). What is "really" going on in human brains, as this is something that no one currently has the slightest clue about.

---

[16] It is indeed amazing what today's spell-checkers (especially in the context of search engines like Google and others) can accomplish in comparison to the spell-checkers of a few years ago. To appreciate this more fully it is worthwhile to check out the contextual features of some of these spell-checkers.

Our opinion is that we stand a real chance of constructing realistic grammars that will encompass millions of variations for a single sentence, if these grammars are based upon the real lexical units (and their variations in turn) that occur in the sentences in question. For an early and insightful discussion of this idea, we recommend Igor Mel'cuk's seminal paper on paraphrases in natural languages, [Mel'cuk, 1988][17]. Maurice Gross has also made similar interesting remarks about variation in elementary sentences in Chapter 1 of [Gross, 1975].

For the analysis of an arbitrary (simple, i.e. elementary) sentence, a grammar needs to take into account at least four ingredients which must be available a priori in the form of devices resembling a lexicon-grammar, in other words, in the form of sophisticated dictionaries:

- The predicate-argument structure of elementary sentences (of course, there is currently no such dictionary of predicate-argument structures for any language).

- The "transformational" properties of the predicate-argument structure (in the sense of Zellig S. Harris and Maurice Gross, these are forthcoming in descriptions of predicates in the style of the verb tables for French initiated by Maurice Gross in the early 1970s, which specify the main argument permutations for each predicate).

---

[17] It should be pointed out that the basic ideas in this paper were already contained in Mel'cuk's PhD thesis in 1975.

- The distributional equivalence classes of its arguments (this needs to be specified, i.e. enumerated in a dictionary of the semantic argument classes of the language).

- The "lexical functions" in the sense of [Mel'čuk, 1998] for the arguments and predicates of the sentences.

- The "grammatical meanings" contained in the sentence.

A grammar, as described for instance in [Guenthner, to appear] then is a mechanism that calculates how a given sentence can be reduced algorithmically to elements described in the four components mentioned above.

1.2 How dictionaries are constructed

We have discussed a variety of dictionary types in the sections above. The only thing that they really have in common is that they have to be constructed on the basis of examining each lexical unit in its own right and by taking into accont their variational properties in corpora.

This is obviously true for the dictionaries of monolexical units for which there are quite a few observations to be made, i.e. concerning the types of information to be coded ranging from morphological descriptions to semantic ones. This task has not yet been been carried out in an adequate manner for any language, in spite of the many useful morphological dictionaries available today.

Even more inspection is necessary to encode the properties of polylexical units; beginning with dictionaries of polylexical nouns we need to construct similar dictionaries for all syntactic categories.

Finally, we face the problem of constructing adequate predicate-argument dictionaries, whose form unfortunately is still relatively unclear. What seems to be the main reason why serious work on this particular dictionary has not gotten off the ground is that there is yet no agreed theoretical basis upon which we might base a *semantic classification* of predicates. The latter problem is in our opinion the most difficult obstacle towards real progress in linguistic analysis.

In spite of the above caveats and difficulties, the most obvious conclusion is simply that constructing the kinds of dictionaries we have described in this chapter will require a concerted (and manual, i.e. intellectual) effort of many hands! This is not a task that a single individual can ever hope to accomplish. But this is no different from what has gone on in every other science during the past centuries: there is a huge need for collaborative effort, agreed to by scientists working more or less with the same perspective on what is necessary for linguistic science to succeed. Compared to the large amounts of money spent on more or less speculative (and not really empirically motivated) undertakings during the past fifty years this objective is not as unreasonable as it might seem at first blush.

1.3   Remarks on the history of lexical automata in NLP

Large-scale dictionary construction efforts are indeed rare. Apart from the well-known, more historically oriented and extremely admirable efforts of the past (e.g. the OED to mention just one of many), modern counterparts can be listed in a few lines. An obvious, and purely pragmatic reason, is to be found in the technical (and maybe also political) support necessary for such undertakings. Describing millions of constructions is not something that one does easily without the right kind of maintenance and acquisition tools. Nevertheless, there are famous examples of systematic efforts. The first one that comes to mind is Salyzniak's morphological dictionary of modern Russian (dating from the 1970s), which has been taken as a source of inspiration and of resources by just about every existing recent implementation of Russian morphological dictionaries until today.

To the best our knowledge, the most extensive effort to describe the simple forms of quite a few languages was inspired by the work at the LADL in Paris[18] and that has led to the construction of serious morphological dictionaries of monolexical and polylexical units as well as many other types of constructions during the past twenty years[19]. These dictionaries are now in use in many industrial applications and are being used by a number of linguistic

---

[18] See: http://ladl.univ-mlv.fr/ and http://infolingu.univ-mlv.fr/english/

[19]   Cf.   the   website   of   the   RELEX-consortium   http://ladl.univ-mlv.fr/Relex/Relex.html.

software companies around the world as well as by many academic institutions[20].

Historically speaking, it seems that (apart from Salyzniak's magnificent manual efforts), the real breakthrough went hand-in-hand with the new possibilities offered by finite-state implementations of large dictionary databases. These can be traced back in part to Liang's thesis [Liang, 1983] on word breaking in TeX in the 1980s and to the first automata-based implementations of large morphological dictionaries at the LADL in 1989. Among other things, these implementations made possible much faster and more robust inspection of corpora for new word forms and this led to faster and faster ways to augment existing dictionaries. Another important source of inspiration and methods in applying finite-state technology techniques emanates from the Xerox research center[21] and has given rise to many applications around the world.

Current implementations of very large electronic dictionaries of the kind discussed here have a look-up speed of a million to several million words per second; the construction algorithms for such large automata have also improved tremendously over the last few

---

[20] They are included (at least in substantial forms) in the grammar writing software tools INTEX/NOOJ [Silberztein, 1993] and Unitex [Paumier, 2003].

[21] Cf. for instance, the many papers by Lauri Kartunnen, see [Beesley, Kartunnen, 2004]; the main emphasis in this group has however been more on the development of algorithmic techniques than on the construction of large dictionaries.

years. While it took several days ten years ago to construct large automata, the same construction now only takes a few minutes.

Since then, combining different approaches, a number of academic institutions and commercial enterprises have paved the way to more and more efficient and wide-scale coverage of the simple forms of many languages. By way of example, let us cite, besides the RELEX-consortium, companies like Teragram, Xerox, Lingsoft, Connexor or Exorbyte[22] and others as organizations who have come to see the value of efficiently represented lexical resources as the best starting point for more advanced applications.

1.4 Types of dictionaries

This book addresses the question of how to construct programs that allow for the efficient representation of dictionary structures that are optimal in the time it takes to build them and the time it takes to execute them on large text data. The methods we discuss are useful for a variety of dictionary types and as we shall see below they are also extendable to more complex lexicographical data types and applications as well.

Finite-state devices, whether it is finite-state automata or finite-state transducers, can represent any large set of strings (given as character sequences) in an optimal way. We will restrict ourselves

---

[22] Exorbyte for instance specializes in algorithms for very rapid approximative search on large lexical databases for use in sophisticated spell-checking and approximate cross-field pattern matching in large structured databases.

in this presentation to so-called acyclic automata (and transducers), i.e. to representations of strings that contain no essential forms of repetition, or recursion or cycles. Essentially we are interested in implementing efficient representations of finite sets of strings, but rather large sets.

Obviously only a small subset of the kinds of constructions we have discussed above fall into this realm in a direct manner. Nevertheless, it is still an open question to what extent the methods we describe here are inherently not amenable to account for the much more complex instances we have mentioned above.

So what are we primarily interested in as far as representing lexicographical facts are concerned?

1.4.1 Monolexical units, polylexical units, fixed phrasal expressions

We first of all want to provide a means to deal with the millions of lexical items that can simply be regarded as a (very) large disjunction of specific instances, i.e. all those elements of a language that are essentially "uninterrupted" sequences of characters[23]. These include all the standard monolexical units, the polylexical units and the "fixed expression" forms.

---

[23] It is important to recall that we are primarily interested in "orthographic" forms in this book and not in other types of representations, e.g. phonetic ones. Cf. [Laporte, 1988] for a detailed discussion "phonetic representations" of words based on an finite-state approach.

We are not concerned with other aspects of the "orthographic" encoding of linguistic entities like character encodings, etc. Obviously, most of what we discuss in what follows can be accommodated if we changed the underlying character representations, in particular the choice of different character encodings, etc.

All these elements will typically consist of a tri-part information structure involving an "observed full form", a base form (the lemma), and an informational part, as mentioned above.

1.4.2 Partial words

Many observed word forms do not occur on their own as independent tokens; instead they always occur as "parts" of polylexical units; these also need to be represented in the dictionary but in a slightly different way from the elements in section 1.4.1.

1.4.3 Mixed words

Any dictionary implementation needs to be specific about the character set it is able to accommodate; typically, this is given as a finite list of admissible characters (in some specific form of encoding). Even though the great majority of elementary forms is restricted to the standard alphabet of the language in question, there are quite a few "non-standard" word forms involving, in addition to the basic alphabet a variety of other characters, e.g. numbers, special symbols like the hyphen, or other orthographic means (e.g.

symbols not normally occurring inside words, like the dollar, euro, pound and other signs.)

Already at the level of simple, partial and mixed words we encounter the quite complicated issue of how to "sort" any such set of lexical items containing various forms of characters and also the discussion of multi-lingual sort issues in [Tran, Maurel, Savary, 2005], particularly on the case of proper names.

1.4.4 Proper names

Last but not least there is also a need for various kinds of proper name dictionaries. Recent research has begun to classify proper names systematically[24]. Apart from the obvious types of proper names like names of persons (first names, last names) and geographical entities, there are many further types that need to be specified. Some can be given in the form of compact lists; others need of course to be specified as local grammars based on their internal syntax and the lexical units they can be composed of (e.g. complete person names, company names and the like)[25]. More importantly, in many languages proper names have a morphology that is quite similar to other parts of the dictionary. This is in

---

[24] See, for instance, [Paik, Liddy, Yu, McKenna, 1996] and [Krstev, Vitas, Maurel, Tran, 2005].

[25] For English, see the bibliography about the MUC Conferences [Chinchor, 1997]. For French, see [Friburger, 2002], [Friburger, Maurel, 2004].

particular true of Slavic languages where all proper names can be highly inflected.

As proper names can make up to over 10% of running text as for instance in journalistic prose [Coates-Stephens, 1993] their treatment is just as important as that of the rest of the vocabulary of language. In addition, as proper names are comparatively easy to categorize in semantic and domain- specific classes, their identification is of great importance for a number of important applications like text classification, information extraction, etc. In some application areas a robust and precise recognition of proper names is for instance necessary to deal with them in the appropriate way, for instance in machine translation where it is critical to know which proper names should be translated (and how) and which not.

1.4.5 Domain-specific dictionaries

It is reasonable to assume that the greatest part of (at least) the nominal vocabulary is to be found in domain-specific dictionaries. For applications in these areas (e.g. medicine or physics) it is of course vital to have access to "controlled" vocabularies, i.e. terminology systems, if one wants to construct useful applications.

There will also be a close connection between linguistic dictionaries representing the vocabulary of a given domain and the classification systems, taxonomies, ontologies and thesauri in these areas. Here a close collaboration of linguists and specialists in the various areas is of course a prerequisite for the construction of lexical resources.

In many domains, mostly in scientific areas, large efforts have already been made to build up large size lexical descriptions of the domains in question. Important examples can be found in medicine, mathematics, economics and others, where various kinds of descriptions are already available (e.g. *Snomed* for medicine). However, most of these vocabularies still need to be put in relation to linguistic dictionaries to provide for a more detailed account of their morphology and semantic behavior. This still remains to be done in most disciplines.

In addition to more scientifically oriented terminological efforts, there have been some attempts to use such extended dictionaries in a number of classification projects on the one hand and in efforts for instance to come to grips with the very large vocabulary used in commerce and more recently in e-commerce interactions (i.e. searches) on the Web. Most e-commerce sites (and also search engines in general) could improve their revenues quite a bit if they had access not only to better morphological but also to large synonym dictionaries which would allow their customers to find the appropriate products in a more efficient manner. It suffices to go to any one of the large universal search engines or to any e-commerce site to be impressed by the low degree of precision and recall due to the high number of approximate or even incorrect searches one can observe.

1.5   Information in dictionaries

We will not go into any detail with respect to the form of electronic dictionaries as far as their structured representation in the maintenance systems that need to be deployed on the one hand is concerned; nor will we discuss the exact nature of the morphological, syntactic, semantic and domain-specific properties of lexical items. A good idea of what is needed can be gleaned from inspecting the electronic dictionaries produced in the LADL tradition or in any of the large dictionary projects at academic and industrial centers around the world[26]. The algorithmic discussion in the main part of this book is compatible with any

As far as morphology is concerned there is no essential difference among the many on-going projects even if the specific encodings still differ a lot in their choice of feature names, etc. There is a lot less agreement in the way semantic properties are encoded (if they are encoded at all) and there is also no agreement about what domains and sub-domains are reasonable candidates for separating the millions of technical terms with which scientific literature and the web abound. This is work that remains to be accomplished.

1.6   Beyond automata: transducers

Finite-state representations of large electronic dictionaries have become the favorite means of implementing large dictionaries

---

[26] The interested reader could consult [Courtois, Silberztein, 1990] and [Silberztein, 1993] for information about the lexical information in the French electronic dictionary system, in particular, the DELAS and the DELAF; [Maier-Meyer, 1995] and [Guenthner, Meier, 1995] for information about the German electronic dictionary CISLEX, and [Blanco, 1997] and [Ranchod, 1999] for corresponding information about the Spanish and Portuguese electronic dictionaries, respectively.

during the past 15 years. In fact, all efficient lexical analysis systems rely on finite-state techniques in one way or another.

In addition to the way finite-state implementations are realized technically, this book also addresses the construction and use of an extension of finite-state representations, called (finite-state) transducers which are essentially finite-state machines that not only recognize word forms but also rewrite them in a specific manner. The most obvious use is to have the transducer output the information attached to a recognized word upon reading it. Which elements of the information are in fact attached to the recognized words depends of course largely on the applications one has in mind. This can go from purely morphological information to much more complex forms of information, as for example the "translation" in another language of the lexical units recognized.

1.7   Transducers and grammars: a unified framework

Transducers have been used mainly for morphological analysis and various disambiguation tasks in the past. In addition to recognizing all the lexical units of a language, whether they are monolexical items or polylexical ones, the next step is to use them for generalized parsing as well. There is an obvious advantage of using the same formalisms for most of the linguistic processing needed to achieve particular practical applications.

Besides extracting meaningful units of meaning at the level of argument structures in natural language sentences (which is what most research on information extraction has concentrated on), the next step is take the use of transducers further to achieve levels of robust and unrestricted parsing. How this can be done was first pioneered by Denis Maurel in his work on the analysis of French temporal adverbs [Maurel, 1989, 1996] and Emmanuel Roche [1993, 1999], Jean Senellart [1998, 1999], and Sébastien Paumier [2003, 2004] in their work on analyzing elementary sentences with (cascaded) transducers based on local grammars automatically generated from analytic descriptions of the transformational patterns of predicative forms (as for instance encoded in the tables of verb properties).

The basic underlying idea is to view a construction table for a given predicate (for instance a specific verb or predicative noun) as spelling out all the ways the predicate can be given together with its arguments. This is quite similar to spelling out the various inflectional forms a verb can assume from a morphological point of view. The syntactic transducer for such a predicate will contain all the various grammatical instantiations (person, number, tense, modality, etc.) together with all the transformational patterns it can occur in. The argument types of the predicates are of course specified in the table as well as all the positions in these patterns where additional material can be inserted.

A particularly impressive example of how very detailed analysis of elementary sentences based on full verbs can be specified is work by the late Maurice Gross on what he calls the "lemmatization of compound verbs" in [Gross, 1999]. This finite-state grammar accounts for practically all instances of preverbal modifications (what is typically called the auxiliary structure of sentences) but goes much beyond the pure modal and temporal modifications of verbs by incorporating practically all forms of preverbal syntactic patterns.

44

The result is a finite-state approach to the analysis of elementary sentences minus their fully spelled out arguments and adverbial modifications that can in fact be regarded as a complete "dictionary" of all the forms an elementary sentence can take[27]. When such a sentential transducer is combined with similar transducers for the arguments and modifier phrases we are very close to complete parses of a very large subset of the grammar (i.e. the elementary sentence patterns) of a language. Complex sentences which are essentially combinations of elementary sentences via "higher order" predicates (i.e. connective phrases) should then become analyzable in much the same way[28].

---

[27] This approach to parsing via uses of cascades of finite-state transducers was pioneered by Emmanuel Roche [1993, 1997]; a related but independent approach can be found in [Abney, 1996].

[28] In [Guenthner, to appear] a "corpus calculus" is presented that assumes a "grammar" to consist of cascades of operations which identify the arguments of elementary sentences via noun phrases and modifier transducers leaving behind them schematic elementary sentential forms that are then reduced to predicate-argument structures on the basis of the recognition of the "lexical functions" and

"grammatical meanings" surrounding the main predicate of the elementary sentence.

2. Introductory Example

2.1 Dictionary

Our introductory example is the recognition of the names of weekdays in text, for example in:

Finally, William will come neither Monday, nor Tuesday, but rather Wednesday or Thursday.

Let us assume that we have available a table like the one in Figure 2.1.

```
Friday
Monday
Saturday
Sunday
Thursday
Tuesday
Wednesday
```

Figure 2.1: The weekdays dictionary

2.2 Trees and automata

We could consider reading the words in the text and to comparing each word with the words in our dictionary (in alphabetic order). It is obvious that this procedure would be costly and would require up to seven comparisons for each word in the text (in our example,

William would only be excluded after having consumed the entire dictionary!).

We would like to know that *William* is not a weekday as soon as we have read the letter *i* without having to compare this with the six weekdays that do not begin with the letter *W*. In order to accomplish this, we can use a structure that is very well-known in computer science, the tree structure, and represent our dictionary as in Figure 2.2; such a tree is called a *lexicographic tree*. All we need to do is to look for the letter *W* starting at the top of the tree (from the left so to speak) and then compare the letter *i* with the letter *e* to ascertain that there is no reason to continue.

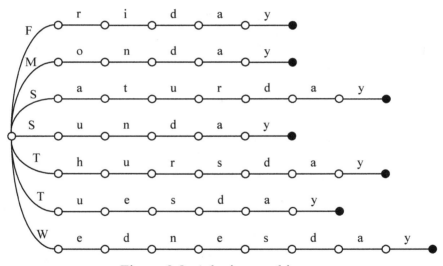

Figure 2.2: A lexicographic tree

In fact, the lexicographic tree is an automaton that recognizes the seven weekdays. Each circle (or *state*) corresponds to reading a letter; each segment (or *transition*) is thus labeled with one of the letters that we want to recognize. The recognition of a word begins with the first state, the *initial state*, and continues until one of the four following situations arises:

1. A failure in the letter-by-letter comparison is encountered, i.e. a given letter in the word fails to match the current letter in the automaton.

2. The word we want to recognize is longer than any word in the automaton.

3. The word we want to recognize comes to an end at an ordinary (i.e. non-final) state.

4. The word comes to an end at a *final state* (in black in the figure).

The first three cases correspond to a failure in the process of recognizing the word; the last case corresponds to success recognition. In this case, we say that the automaton in Figure 2.2 *recognizes* the word we want to check.

This automaton contains fifty-one states (including one initial state and seven final states) and fifty transitions.

2.3 Deterministic automata

Let us continue with this example. We take the word *Sunday* and continue with our automaton. What should we do? We have two transitions labeled with the letter *S*! We assume of course that at this point in the analysis, we have read only the first letter of the word, and that in the automaton the only transitions available are those that begin at the initial state. If we take the first transition, the comparison of the letter *u* with the letter *a* leads to a failure, but this does not end our analysis. We must backtrack now, which presupposes that we have stored the path followed up to now, and restart with the second transition from the initial state labeled with the letter *S*.

This is obviously very costly, both in terms of the memory space needed to store the path taken up to now and to keep track of all the alternative choices we encountered, and in terms of the computation time used for many backtracking steps that need to be taken.

In order to overcome these difficulties, it suffices to allow only one transition to emanate from a state for a given label. This gives rise to the notion of a *deterministic automaton*. The automaton in Figure 2.3 is a deterministic automaton that recognizes the seven weekdays. We have eliminated the choice between the two *S*'s and between the two *T*'s by shifting one state to the right.

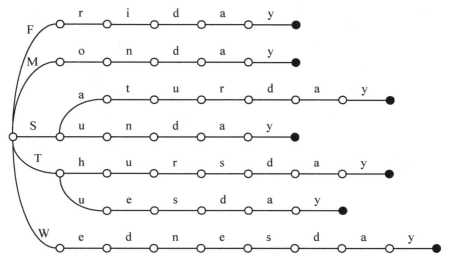

Figure 2.3: A deterministic automaton

This automaton has two states and two transitions less than the automaton in Figure 2.2. Observe that the last automaton still looks like a lexicographic tree, but this is not necessarily the case and will change in the following examples.

2.4 Minimal deterministic automata

Observe now that the formation of these seven words is not due to chance: etymologically they retain some trace of the Latin word *dies* (*day*). This shows up in the fact that they share the same final letters. This leads to the idea that we might be able to reduce the number of states from left to right as well.

For instance, the letter *y* shows up at the end of the weekdays and corresponds, in the automaton in Figure 2.3, to seven transitions. Why not replace these with a single transition? The same holds for the *a* and the *d*. Moreover, the letter *s* is shared by three words (two of whom also share an *e*) and the letter *n* by two words: this should be taken into account as well. When there are no more ways to merge the end of words, we say that the deterministic automaton is *minimal*.

In Figure 2.4 we have such an automaton for the recognition of the seven weekdays. We can show that this automaton is (up to renumbering the states) unique. We can thus speak of the minimal deterministic automaton that is equivalent to the automata in Figure 2.2 and Figure 2.3.

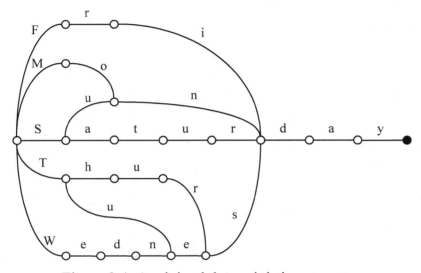

Figure 2.4: A minimal deterministic automaton

This automaton contains twenty-one states and twenty-six transitions. We have gone from fifty-one states in the automaton in Figure 2.2 to twenty-one states in the automaton in Figure 2.4, which represents a reduction of 58.8 %.

2.5   Recognizing and informing

Recognizing a word is one thing, but in general we are also interested in associating some information about the word from the dictionary. This could be, for instance, a grammatical class (noun, verb, etc.), inflectional information (feminine singular, past tense) or semantic information (weekday, name of a month, etc.) as well as many other types of information forthcoming from the intended application domain.

One option might be to construct individual automata for the available information categories and to test all of the words with respect to each of those automata. This would of course require storing a large number of automata, which would take large amounts of memory and computation time. We will present two other solutions for the association of various types of information to the recognition of words.

The first solution, multi-terminal automata (section 2.6), consists in putting this information in the final states of the automaton; the second solution, transducers, in spreading out this information at various places in the automaton (section 2.7).

2.6 Multi-terminal automata

We modify the dictionary in Figure 2.1 by indicating for each of the weekdays whether or not it is a working day or a day off. The table in Figure 2.5 now contains two columns, the input (to be recognized) and the output (the information to be written).

Friday	Working day
Monday	Working day
Saturday	Day off
Sunday	Day off
Thursday	Working day
Tuesday	Working day
Wednesday	Working day

Figure 2.5: Which day do we work?

The automaton in Figure 2.6 is similar to the previous automaton with one small difference: it has two final states labeled *Working day* and *Day off*. Such an automaton is called a *Moore machines*[29] or a *multi-terminal automaton*[30].

---

[29] See [Watson, 1995].

[30] See [Revuz, 1991].

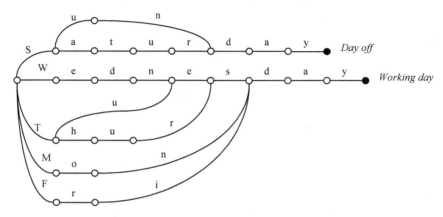

Figure 2.6: A multi-terminal automaton

In this kind of automata, the left-to-right reduction operates obviously only on words in the same class. The efficiency of this model thus requires a much-reduced number of classes compared to the words in the dictionary. Nevertheless we can observe here a reduction of 49.0% in the number of states: twenty-six states in Figure 2.6 compared to fifty-one states in Figure 2.2.

2.7 Transducers

As we have already remarked, we lose the possibility of reducing the number of states from left to right. We will therefore assume that information can be emitted not only in final states, but also by internal transitions.

We can thus view a transducer as an automaton "emitting" symbols at every transition as well as at final states. We now rewrite the weekday example in Figure 2.7. Observe that since the information associated with *Saturday* and *Sunday* is the same, it is possible to "factorize" on the initial *S*. The same holds for the words *Thursday* and *Tuesday*.

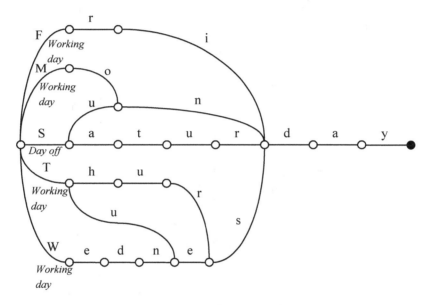

Figure 2.7: A first transducer

This transducer recognizes the same words and emits the same information as the multi-terminal automaton in Figure 2.6, but its underlying automaton is an exact copy of the automaton in Figure 2.4. Such a situation is in fact ideal, unfortunately, this correspondence between automata and transducers is not always possible as we shall show later. Nevertheless, a transducer is in general less voluminous than a multi-terminal[31] automaton.

Consider another example: assume that the transducer should yield information concerning the date of February 29 beginning in the year 2004: We might want to know which weekday is February 29? (Figure 2.8).

February 29	
Sunday	2004
Friday	2008
Wednesday	2012
Monday	2016
Saturday	2020
Thursday	2024
Tuesday	2028

Figure 2.8: What weekday is February 29?

We will put these years as output of the automaton in Figure 2.4. In the same way that we have factorized the *S* in *Saturday* and *Sunday*, we can factorize the sequence *20* corresponding to these two weekdays. The same holds for *Thursday* and *Tuesday*: we can factorize the sequence *202*. This leads us to the transducer in

---

[31] One can consult in this connection [Mohri, 1996] for a dictionary of over six hundred thousand entries.

Figure 2.9 where the final information is obtained in a "piecewise" fashion.

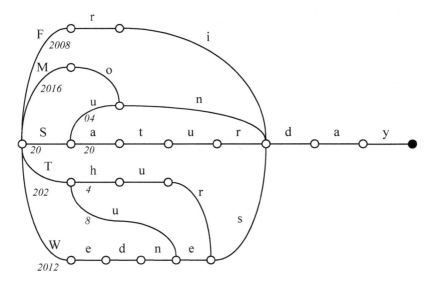

Figure 2.9: A second transducer

2.8 Another linguistic example: the verb forms

For instance, if we want to recognize all the forms of a regular verb, like *to contract, to edit, to head, to tend,* we have just to recognize four inflectional forms (*0, s, ed, ing*), as on Figure 2.10.

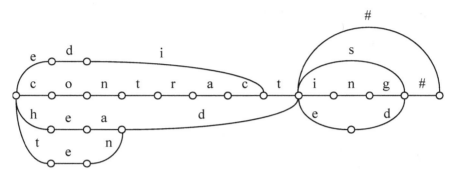

Figure 2.10: Regular English verb forms

We can also represent verbs with prefixes[32], like *to code, to decode, to recode, to compose, to decompose, to recompose, to fuse, to defuse, to refuse, to merge, to demerge, to remerge* (Figure 2.11).

---

[32] We use the term *prefix*, even it is not a prefix in the ordinary sense of the word.

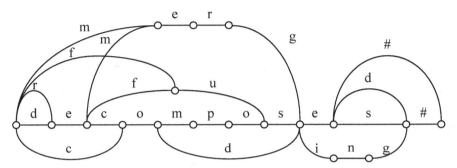

Figure 2.11: More complex English verb forms

In French, the most common paradigm is the one of the verb *chanter* (*to sing*): For instance, three hundred and four French verbs follow this paradigm among the six hundred and fifteen French verbs beginning with the letter *a*. This verb has forty-nine simple tenses and thirty-nine are different. Figure 2.12 presents the verbs *chanter* (*to sing*), *tailler* (*to carve*), *enchanter* (*to delight*), *déchanter* (*to become disenchanted*), *entailler* (*to cut into*) and *détailler* (*to detail*) in the first and second person of the plural, present, future and conditional tenses.

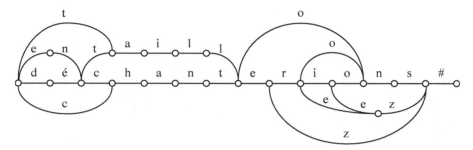

Figure 2.12: Some French verb forms

French has a quite a big number of verb forms, but Slavic languages (among others) use case for nouns and adjectives, so these languages also have a great number of noun forms and great number of adjective forms! The use of minimal deterministic automata thus provides an interesting means for considerably reducing the size of the dictionary.

3. Definitions

3.1 Monoid

3.1.1 Definition

A *monoid* is a set $\mathcal{M}$ together with an associative operation $*$; if there exists a neutral element, designated by ε, then the monoid is called *free* (Figure 3.1).

$(\mathcal{M}, *)$ is a free monoid iff

$*$ is an internal operation: $\forall\, x, y \in \mathcal{M}, x*y \in \mathcal{M}$

$*$ is associative: $\forall\, x, y, z \in \mathcal{M}, (x*y)*z = x*(y*z)$

$\mathcal{M}$ contains a neutral element ε: $\forall\, x \in \mathcal{M}, x*\varepsilon = \varepsilon*x = x$

Figure 3.1: Definition of a free monoid

3.1.2 Concatenation

Let $\mathcal{L}$ be a finite non-empty set (the letters); we call $\mathcal{L}^*$, the set consisting of the empty string ε and all finite sequences of elements of $\mathcal{L}$.

For example:

- If $\mathcal{A} = \{a\}$, $\mathcal{A}^* = \{\varepsilon, a, aa, aaa, aaaa, ...\}$.

- If $\mathcal{A} = \{a, b\}$, $\mathcal{A}^* = \{\varepsilon, a, b, aa, ab, ba, bb, aaa, ...\}$.

Let m_1 and m_2 be two elements of $\mathcal{A}^*$; we call *concatenation* the internal operation which associates the sequence m_1m_2 with the pair (m_1, m_2) from the Cartesian product of $\mathcal{A}^*$ and $\mathcal{A}^*$ (Figure 3.2).

The concatenation operation is defined by

$$\mathcal{A}^* \times \mathcal{A}^* \to \mathcal{A}^*$$
$$(m_1, m_2) \to m_1m_2$$

Figure 3.2: Concatenation

For example, given $\mathcal{A} = \{a, b\}$, if $m_1 = ab$ and $m_2 = ba$, then $m_1m_2 =$ abba. The set $\mathcal{A}^*$, together with the concatenation operation is a free monoid.

3.2 Automata

3.2.1 Definition

An *finite-state automaton*[33] over $\mathcal{L}$ is a five-tuple $\mathcal{A} = (\mathcal{Q}, \mathcal{L}, q_0, \mathcal{F}, \delta)$ where:

- $\mathcal{Q}$ is a non-empty finite set of states

- $\mathcal{L}$ is a non-empty set of letters (the alphabet)

- q_0 is an element of $\mathcal{Q}$ (the initial state)

- $\mathcal{F}$ is a non-empty subset of $\mathcal{Q}$ (the final states)

- δ is a relation defined from $\mathcal{Q} \times \mathcal{L}$ to $\mathcal{Q}$ (the transitions).

When we say that δ is a simple relation from $\mathcal{Q} \times \mathcal{L}$ to $\mathcal{Q}$ we mean that an element in $\mathcal{Q} \times \mathcal{L}$ can have no image under δ, or only one or several. We use $\delta(q, \ell)$ to refer to the set:

$$\delta(q, \ell) = \{q' \in \mathcal{Q} / (q, \ell, q') \text{ is a transition in the automaton } \mathcal{A}\}$$

We say that an element $\ell_1 \ell_2 \ldots \ell_n$ of the monoid $\mathcal{L}^*$ is recognized by the automaton $\mathcal{A}$ if and only if it corresponds to a sequence of n

---

[33] In the restricted context of this text, we will from now on refer to *a finite state automaton* with the simpler term *automaton*.

transitions (labeled respectively by ℓ_1, ℓ_2,... and ℓ_n), beginning with the initial state q_0 and ending with the final state p_n (Figure 3.3).

$$\ell_1\ell_2...\ell_n \text{ is recognized by } \mathcal{A} \text{ iff:}$$

$$\exists\, p_0, p_1,..., p_n \in \mathcal{Q}, \text{ such that:}$$
$$\forall\, i=0, 1, ..., \text{n-1}, p_{i+1} \in \delta(p_i, \ell_{i+1})$$
$$p_0 = q_0$$
$$p_n \in \mathcal{F}$$

Figure 3.3: Recognition of a word by an automaton

The set of elements in $\mathcal{L}^*$ recognized by $\mathcal{A}$ is called the *language* defined by $\mathcal{A}$. It is designated by $L(\mathcal{A})$.

3.2.2 Example

Let us return to the example of the weekdays with the automaton in Figure 2.4, page 53. Figure 3.4 presents this automaton again; we have simply enumerated the different states.

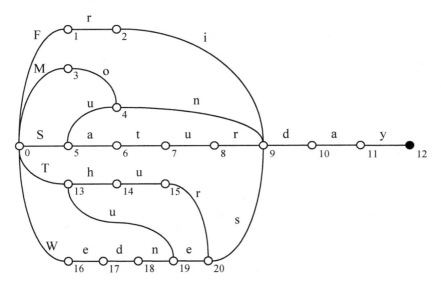

Figure 3.4: An automaton for the days of the week

Here we have:

$\mathcal{Q}$ = {0, 1, 2, 3, 4, 5, 6, 7, 8, 9, 10, 11, 12, 13, 14, 15, 16, 17, 18, 19, 20}

$\mathcal{A}$ = {F, M, S, T, W, a, d, e, h, i, n, o, r, s, t, u, y}

q_0 = 0

$\mathcal{F}$ = {12}

67

$\delta(0, F)=\{1\}$	$\delta(0, M)=\{3\}$	$\delta(0, S)=\{5\}$	$\delta(0, T)=\{13\}$	$\delta(0, W)=\{16\}$
$\delta(1, r)=\{2\}$	$\delta(2, i)=\{9\}$	$\delta(3, o)=\{4\}$	$\delta(4, n)=\{9\}$	$\delta(5, a)=\{6\}$
$\delta(5, u)=\{4\}$	$\delta(6, t)=\{7\}$	$\delta(7, u)=\{8\}$	$\delta(8, r)=\{9\}$	$\delta(9, d)=\{10\}$
$\delta(10, a)=\{11\}$	$\delta(11, y)=\{12\}$	$\delta(13, h)=\{14\}$	$\delta(13, u)=\{19\}$	$\delta(14, u)=\{15\}$
$\delta(15, r)=\{20\}$	$\delta(16, e)=\{17\}$	$\delta(17, d)=\{18\}$	$\delta(18, n)=\{19\}$	$\delta(19, e)=\{20\}$
$\delta(20, s)=\{9\}$				

The automaton recognizes for instance *Sunday* via the sequence:

$$5 \in \delta(0, S), 4 \in \delta(5, u), 9 \in \delta(4, n), 10 \in \delta(9, d), 11 \in \delta(10, a), 12 \in \delta(11, y)$$
$$\text{and } 12 \in \mathcal{F}$$

and the language recognized by $\mathcal{A}$ is made up exactly of the seven weekdays:

$$L(\mathcal{A})=\{\text{Friday, Monday, Saturday, Sunday, Thursday, Tuesday, Wednesday}\}$$

3.2.3 Empty transitions

Let us exchange the dictionary of weekdays with a dictionary containing polylexical units. The graphical form of these words is not always well determined; sometimes the hyphen is facultative and sometimes it is replaced by a space or a monolexical unit[34]. Let us take as an example the dictionary in Figure 3.5.

---

[34] For an extensive treatment of the forms of compound words with a hyphen in French see [Mathieu-Colas, 1988].

sub
sub-group
sub group
subgroup
sub-groups
sub groups
subgroups
subs

Figure 3.5: A dictionary with the different graphical forms of the same word

In order to recognize these words, why not directly write in the automaton that the hyphen and the space are optional? To accomplish this, it suffices to slightly modify the definition of the function δ (section 3.2.1, page 65); we define an automaton with ε-transitions with the five-tuple $\mathcal{A}=(\mathcal{Q}, \mathcal{A}, q_0, \mathcal{F}, \delta)$ where:

- δ is a relation defined from $\mathcal{Q} \times (\mathcal{A} \cup \{\varepsilon\})$ in $\mathcal{Q}$.

We now have empty transitions, labeled by ε, as in Figure 3.6 (the symbol $\square$ replaces the *space* character).

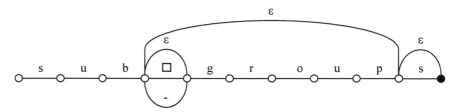

Figure 3.6: An automaton with ε–transitions

3.2.4 Eliminating empty transitions

Even though the introduction of empty transitions can simplify many linguistic descriptions, it complicates things from a computational point of view. In fact, an automaton with ε-transitions is always equivalent to an automaton that does not have any, as we saw in section 4.1, page 79.

In order to transform this automaton, a first idea consists in replacing the ε-transitions that lead to a final state by intermediary final states (i.e. equipped with outgoing transitions) as in Figure 3.7. A final state without outgoing transitions will be called *terminal*.

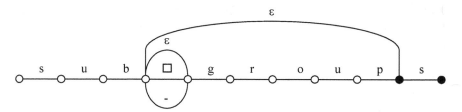

Figure 3.7: An equivalent automaton with ε-transitions and non-final terminal states

We can then eliminate the last ε-transitions by replacing them with transitions that are identical to those of the state that they reach. We obtain the automaton in Figure 3.8 that recognizes the same language as the automata in Figure 3.6 and in Figure 3.7.

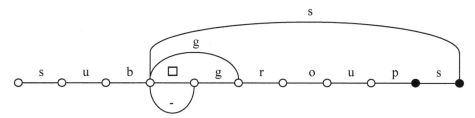

Figure 3.8: An equivalent automaton
without ε-transitions, but with non-terminal final states

It is however inconvenient to introduce intermediary final states: Because there is the additional need to regulate the status (final or non-final) of states.

Another idea is to use an *end-of-word character* (#) and a single final state. Let us again modify the definition of the function δ (section 3.2.1, page 65, and section 3.2.3, page 68):

- δ is a relation defined from $\mathbf{2} \times (\mathbf{4} \cup \{\varepsilon, \#\})$ to $\mathbf{2}$.

The automaton in Figure 3.6 is now given in the form of Figure 3.9 or Figure 3.10.

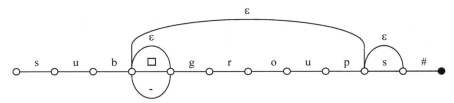

Figure 3.9: An equivalent automaton with ε-transitions and an end-of-word character

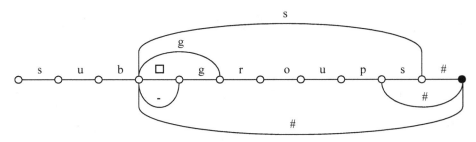

Figure 3.10: An equivalent automaton without ε-transitions, but with an end-of-word character

It is the last representation that we will use in what follows. An *automaton* is defined as a five-tuple $\mathcal{A}=(\mathcal{Q}, \mathcal{L}, q_0, q_1, \delta)$ where:

- $\mathcal{Q}$ is a non-empty set of states

- $\mathcal{L}$ is a non-empty set of letters (the alphabet)

- q_0 is an element in $\mathcal{Q}$ (the initial state)

- q_1 is an element in $\mathcal{Q}$ (the final state)

- δ is a relation defined from $\mathcal{Q} \times (\mathcal{L} \cup \{\varepsilon, \#\})$ to $\mathcal{Q}$ (the transitions).

3.2.5 Acyclic automata

In all the previous examples, our automata, which are designed to recognize sequences of words, do not contain any infinite paths. In other words, they have no cycles. In such cases we speak of *acyclic* automata. In the following chapters, all our automata will therefore be acyclic.

3.3 Transducers

3.3.1 Definition

A *finite-state-p-sub-sequential transducer* [35] over $\mathcal{A}$ is a seven-tuple $\mathcal{T}=(\mathcal{Q}, \mathcal{A}, \mathcal{S}, q_0, q_1, \delta, \lambda)$[36] where:

- $\mathcal{Q}$ is a non-empty finite set of states

- $\mathcal{A}$ and $\mathcal{S}$ are non-empty finite sets of letters (the input and the output alphabets, respectively)

- q_0 is an element of $\mathcal{Q}$ (the initial state)

- q_1 is an element of $\mathcal{Q}$ (the final state)

- δ is a function defined from $\mathcal{Q} \times (\mathcal{A} \cup \{\#\})$ to $\mathcal{Q}$ (the transition function)

- λ is a function defined from $\mathcal{Q} \times (\mathcal{A} \cup \{\#\})$ to $(\mathcal{S} \cup \{|\})^*$ (the transition output function).

---

[35] Simply called a *transducer* in what follows.

[36] In the case where we choose to work with a representation with non-terminal final states, we need to add to this definition a function σ defined from $\mathcal{F}$ to $(\mathcal{S} \cup \{|\})^*$ (the output function for final states). If we replace the function λ with the function σ, the transducer we obtain is in fact a *multi-terminal automaton* over $\mathcal{A}$.

To say that δ is a function from $\mathcal{Q} \times (\mathcal{A} \cup \{\#\})$ to $\mathcal{Q}$ means that an element in $\mathcal{Q} \times (\mathcal{A} \cup \{\#\})$ can have no image or one and only one image with respect to δ. We use $\delta(q, \ell)$ to refer to that unique image. The same holds for λ. We do not allow ε-transitions for this type of transducer.

The automaton $(\mathcal{Q}, \mathcal{A}, q_0, q_1, \delta)$ is called the *underlying automaton* of the transducer $\mathcal{T}$.

We will see in section 7.1, page 147, that the symbol $|$ is used only to indicate different output for the same word and that it occurs only in the last output of the word being read; this limits the computation of the output associated with a word to two cases:

1. The last output is an element in S^*; we concatenate the outputs of the transitions.

2. Otherwise, we concatenate every "piece" of the last output.

Let us define a function Λ from $(S \cup \{|\})^*$ in $(S \cup \{|\})^*$ by:

$\forall o_1 \in (S \cup \{|\})^*, \forall o_2 \in (S \cup \{|\})^*,$

  if $o_1 \in S^*$ and $o_2 \in S^*$,

    then $\Lambda(o_1, o_2) = o_1 o_2$

  if $o_1 \in S^*$ and $o_2 \notin S^*$,

    with $\exists t_0, t_1, ..., t_n \in S^*$, such that $o_2 = t_1 | t_2 \cdots t_{n-1} | t_n$,

      then $\Lambda(o_1, o_2) = o_1 t_1 | o_1 t_2 \cdots o_1 t_{n-1} | o_1 t_n$

  otherwise $\Lambda(o_1, o_2) = \varepsilon$

We now define the output of an element $l_1l_2...l_n$ of the monoid $\mathcal{L}^*$ recognized by the transducer $\mathcal{T}$ (Figure 3.11).

$l_1l_2...l_n$ is recognized by $\mathcal{T}$
and has as output $s=\Lambda(s_1s_2...s_{n-1}, s_n)$ if and only if:

$\exists\ p_0, p_1,..., p_n \in \mathcal{Q}$, such that:

$\forall\ i=0, 1, ..., n-1, \delta(p_i, l_{i+1})=p_{i+1}$

$\forall\ i=0, 1, ..., n-1, \lambda(p_i, l_{i+1})=s_{i+1}$

$p_0=q_0$

$p_n=q_1$

Figure 3.11: Word recognized by a transducer

3.3.2 Example

Let us look at the second example of a transducer in Figure 2.9, page 59. Figure 3.12 shows a transducer with a number for each state.

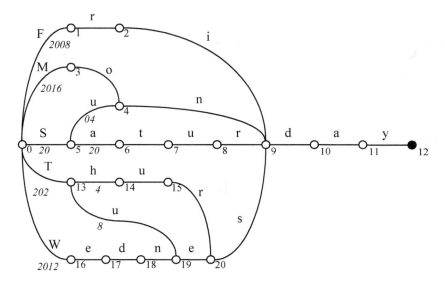

Figure 3.12: A transducer for February 29

Here we have:

$\mathcal{Q}$={0, 1, 2, 3, 4, 5, 6, 7, 8, 9, 10, 11, 12, 13, 14, 15, 16, 17, 18, 19, 20}

$\mathcal{A}$={F, M, S, T, W, a, d, e, h, i, n, o, r, s, t, u, y}

$\mathcal{S}$={0, 1, 2, 4, 6, 8}

q_0=0

q_i=12

δ(0, F)={1}	δ(0, M)={3}	δ(0, S)={5}	δ(0, T)={13}	δ(0, W)={16}
δ(1, r)={2}	δ(2, i)={9}	δ(3, 0)={4}	δ(4, n)={9}	δ(5, a)={6}
δ(5, u)={4}	δ(6, t)={7}	δ(7, u)={8}	δ(8, r)={9}	δ(9, d)={10}
δ(10, a)={11}	δ(11, y)={12}	δ(13, h)={14}	δ(13, u)={19}	δ(14, u)={15}
δ(15, r)={20}	δ(16, e)={17}	δ(17, d)={18}	δ(18, n)={19}	δ(19, e)={20}
δ(20, s)={9}				

λ(0, F)=2008	λ(0, M)=2016	λ(0, S)=20
λ(0, T)=202	λ(0, W)=2012	λ(5, a)=20
λ(5, u)=04	λ(13, h)=4	λ(13, u)=8

The transducer τ recognizes for instance the word *Sunday* on the basis of the same sequence of transitions as in section 3.2.2, page 66; it also outputs the following information:

$$\lambda(0, S)\lambda(5,u) = \Lambda(20, 04) = 2004$$

If we add that February 29 2000 was on Tuesday, we have to modify:

$$\lambda(0, T)=20, \lambda(13, h)=24 \text{ and } \lambda(13, u)=00|28$$

In this case, the output of *Tuesday* is:

$$\lambda(0, T)\lambda(13,u) = \Lambda(20, 00|28) = 2000|2028$$

4. Determinism

4.1 The deletion of ε-transitions

Consider again the example in Figure 3.6, page 70 (Figure 4.1).

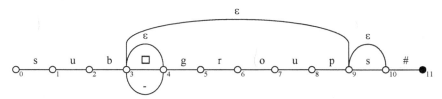

Figure 4.1: An automaton with ε-transitions

Figure 4.2 presents a *transition table* for this automaton: the lines contain the states of the automaton, and the columns the different transitions. The states reached by a pair (*p*, a) are placed at the intersection of line p and column a. In fact, this table is almost empty, which is of little interest as far as the representation of an automaton is concerned except for its pedagogical use in designing our algorithm[37].

---

[37] And except if the input alphabet is very small, for example the four letters of the genome (see [Crochemore, Vérin, 1997]).

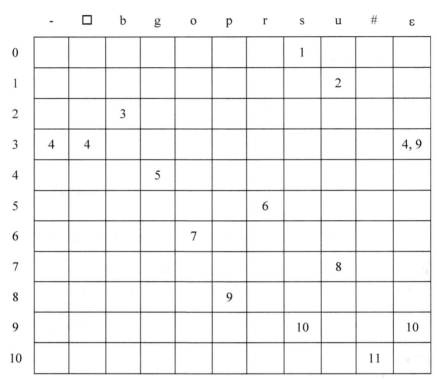

	-	□	b	g	o	p	r	s	u	#	ε
0								1			
1									2		
2			3								
3	4	4									4, 9
4				5							
5							6				
6					7						
7									8		
8						9					
9								10			10
10										11	

Figure 4.2: A transition table

We will delete the last column of this table:

- Since we find 4 and 9 in the cell (3, ε), we copy lines 4 and 9 in line 3.

- However, by doing this, we also add the 10 of cell (9, ε) into cell (3, ε), and this forces us to continue our copying operation with line 10 to line 3.

- Finally, due to the presence of this 10 in cell (9, ε), we copy line 10 to line 9.

We thus obtain a new transition table (Figure 4.3) which corresponds to an automaton without ε-transitions that recognizes the same language (Figure 4.4).

	-	□	b	g	o	p	r	s	u	#
0								1		
1									2	
2			3							
3	4	4		5				10		11
4				5						
5							6			
6					7					
7									8	
8						9				
9								10		11
10										11

Figure 4.3: The modified table

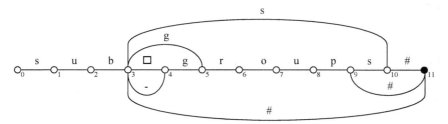

Figure 4.4: An equivalent automaton without ε-transitions

4.2 Determinism

4.2.1 Definition

An automaton $A=(2, \mathcal{A}, q_0, q_1, \delta)$, without ε-transitions, is called deterministic if and only if all the transition labels from any state are distinct. This is equivalent to noting that δ is a function defined from $2 \times (\mathcal{A} \cup \{\#\})$ to 2.

4.2.2 Theorem

Given an automaton A, there exists a deterministic automaton A that recognizes the same language [Myhill, 1957][38].

---

[38] One can consult [Hopcroft, Ullman, 1979] and [Watson, 1995] for more information.

83

4.2.3 Example

Consider the previous example (Figure 4.4). One infers from the transition table that the automaton is deterministic, since there is only one state per cell. Let us take another dictionary (Figure 4.5) and another automaton (Figure 4.6) with its transition table (Figure 4.7) as an example.

race
rage
rice

Figure 4.5: A dictionary with three words

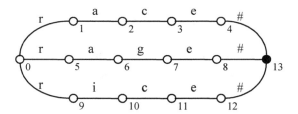

Figure 4.6: A non-deterministic automaton
recognizing these three words

	a	c	e	i	g	r	#
0						1, 5, 9	
1	2						
2		3					
3			4				
4							13
5	6						
6					7		
7			8				
8							13
9				10			
10		11					
11			12				
12							13

Figure 4.7: The transition table for this automaton

Since the cell (0, r) contains three states, we will create a new line representing a new state, the state 1_5_9, obtained by merging the lines 1, 5 and 9 (Figure 4.8).

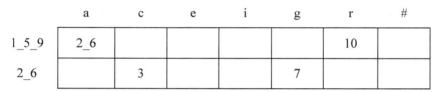

	a	c	e	i	g	r	#
0						1_5_9	
1_5_9	2, 6			10			

Figure 4.8: The first modifications

This operation must be repeated as we now find two new states in the same cell in this new line. We therefore merge lines 2 and 6 (Figure 4.9).

	a	c	e	i	g	r	#
1_5_9	2_6					10	
2_6		3			7		

Figure 4.9: The next modifications

This procedure is necessarily finite[39]. We can observe moreover (but this is not always the case as we will see in section 4.3), that the states 1, 2, 5, 6 and 9 are no longer reachable, since they don't appear in the table; this will allow us to delete these five lines. Finally, we obtain the table in Figure 4.10 and the equivalent deterministic automaton (Figure 4.11).

---

[39] Since the number of lines is always inferior to the cardinal of the set of subsets of $\mathbf{2}$, that is 2^n, if n is the cardinal of the set $\mathbf{2}$.

	a	c	e	i	g	r	#
0						1_5_9	
3			4				
4							13
7			8				
8							13
10		11					
11			12				
12							13
1_5_9	2_6			10			
2_6		3			7		

Figure 4.10: The resulting table

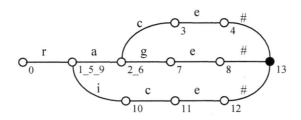

Figure 4.11: An equivalent deterministic automaton

87

4.3 The number of states after determinization

When we compare the automata in Figure 4.6 and in Figure 4.11, one is led to think that determinization entails a reduction (from left to right) of the number of states. Indeed, the automaton in Figure 4.6 has fourteen states whereas the one in Figure 4.11 has only eleven.

In fact, this is one among many situations because during determinization, all cases may present themselves: reduction, equivalence or increase in the number of states.

Let us give an example where the number of states remains identical starting with the non-deterministic automaton in Figure 4.12. This automaton recognizes the three words *tab*, *tub* and *sub*.

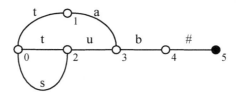

Figure 4.12: A non-deterministic automaton recognizing *tab*, *tub* and *sub*

This automaton has six states. The determinization table is given in the table in Figure 4.13 (line 1 disappears, because state 1 is not reached.).

	a	b	s	t	u	#
0			2	1, 2		
1	3					
2					3	
3		4				
4						5
1_2	3				3	

Figure 4.13: The determinization table

The deterministic corresponding automaton has only six states. This automaton is shown in Figure 4.14.

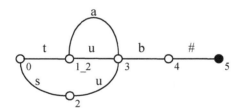

Figure 4.14: A deterministic automaton
with the same number of states

On the other hand, if we also want to recognize the word *lab*, we will need to modify the initial automaton by adding a transition, as in Figure 4.15, and the result will be different!

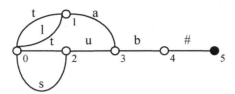

Figure 4.15: A non-deterministic automaton
recognizing *tab*, *tub*, *sub* and *lab*

This automaton still has six states. The determinization table is
given in Figure 4.16. It differs from the previous one only in the
addition of column *l*; but now the presence of state 1 in this
column, absent from the table in Figure 4.13, forces us to retain this
state.

	a	b	l	s	t	u	#
0			1	2	1, 2		
1	3						
2						3	
3		4					
4							5
1_2	3					3	

Figure 4.16: The new determinization table

The corresponding deterministic automaton now has seven states as
we can see in Figure 4.17.

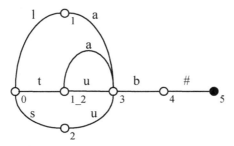

Figure 4.17: A deterministic automaton with a larger number of states

4.4 Exercises

Go back to the example of Figure 2.11, page 61, considering the prefixes *de-*, *re-* and the suffixes *-s*, *-d* as optional: *to code, to decode, to recode, to compose, to decompose, to recompose, to fuse, to defuse, to refuse, to merge, to demerge, to remerge,* as in Figure 4.18.

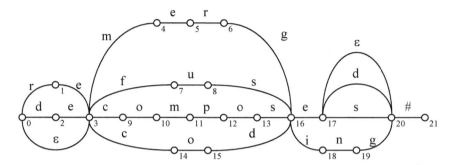

Figure 4.18: Optional prefixes and suffixes

1.   Delete the ε-transitions, as in section 4.1, page 79.

2.   Determinize the resulting automaton, as in section 4.2.3, page 84.

5. Minimization

5.1 The minimization of acyclic automata

5.1.1 Theorem

Given a deterministic automaton $\mathcal{A}$, there exists one and only one minimal deterministic automaton $\mathcal{A}$ which recognizes the same language (up to renumbering of the states) [Moore, 1956].

One easily deduces from this theorem and the previous one (section 4.2.1, page 83) the following corollary:

Given an automaton $\mathcal{A}$, there exists one and only one minimal deterministic $\mathcal{A}$ that recognizes the same language (up to renumbering of the states).

5.1.2 The transition table

As above, we shall consider the transition table of the automaton. All the lines in Figure 4.3, page 82, are distinct: it is thus impossible to minimize the automaton in Figure 4.4, page 83, which is already the minimal deterministic automaton recognizing the dictionary on page 69. On the other hand, in Figure 4.10, page 87, we find three identical states (the lines 4, 8 and 12) that we will be able to merge (Figure 5.1).

	a	c	e	i	g	r	#
0						1_5_9	
3			4_8_12				
7			4_8_12				
10		11					
11			4_8_12				
1_5_9	2_6			10			
2_6		3			7		
4_8_12							13

Figure 5.1: The merging of 4, 8 and 12

Now it is lines 3, 7 and 11 that we will be able to merge (Figure 5.2). There are no more identical lines: we have obtained (Figure 5.3) the minimal deterministic automaton recognizing the dictionary in Figure 3.5, page 69.

	a	c	e	i	g	r	#
0						1_5_9	
10		3_7_11					
1_5_9	2_6			10			
2_6		3_7_11			3_7_11		
4_8_12							13
3_7_11			4_8_12				

Figure 5.2: The merge of lines 3, 7 and 11

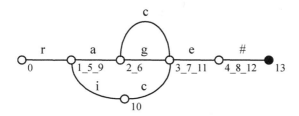

Figure 5.3: The corresponding minimal deterministic automaton

This algorithm seems to work, but one practical question arises immediately: how to find the identical lines? We can take the first line and compare it to all the others, eventually merge one of the lines we find with the first, and then begin again with the second line. For an automaton with a large number of states, this turns out to be unrealistic. We need to find another way to reduce the number of lines to compare.

5.1.3 Height of a state

Dominique Revuz has proposed an answer to this problem, which we are going to describe briefly [Revuz, 1992][40]. This algorithm uses a function that associates with each state the maximal number of transitions necessary to reach a final state. Revuz calls this number the *height* of a state (Figure 5.4).

Let $\mathcal{A}=(\mathcal{Q}, \mathcal{L}, q_0, q_1, \delta)$ be a deterministic acyclic automaton

$\forall \, p \in \mathcal{Q}$, Height$(p)$=Max(n)

where n is defined by:
$\exists \, p_1, p_2, ..., p_{n+1} \in \mathcal{Q}, \exists \, \ell_1, \ell_2, ..., \ell_n \in \mathcal{L}$, such that
$\qquad \forall \, i=1, 2, ..., n, \delta(p_i, \ell_i)=p_{i+1}$
with:
$p_1 = p$
$p_{n+1} = q_1$

Figure 5.4: Definition of the height of a state

---

[40] A minimization algorithm exists for arbitrary automata [Hopcroft, 1971], see [Hopcroft, Ullman, 1979] and [Berstel, Carton, 2003]. In the case of acyclic automata, the algorithm in [Revuz, 1992] is the most efficient.

5.1.4 *Example*

We return to the example in Figure 4.11, page 87. The set of states is:

$$\mathcal{Z} = \{0, 1\_5\_9, 2\_6, 3, 4, 7, 8, 10, 11, 12, 13\}$$

We will create a partition of $\mathcal{Z}$ by separating the states on the basis of their height. We then obtain six classes:

$\mathcal{Z}_0 = \{13\}$	$\mathcal{Z}_1 = \{4, 8, 12\}$
$\mathcal{Z}_2 = \{3, 7, 11\}$	$\mathcal{Z}_3 = \{2\_6, 10\}$
$\mathcal{Z}_4 = \{1\_5\_9\}$	$\mathcal{Z}_5 = \{0\}$

It is now possible to put each of the lines in the transition table. To do this, we proceed according to the decreasing order of heights by merging, if this is possible, the states of $\mathcal{Z}_0$, then of $\mathcal{Z}_1$, of $\mathcal{Z}_2$, etc. Two states with the same height can then be merged if the corresponding lines in the transition table are the same, that is, if the transitions which come from them lead to the same states with the same labels.

This algorithm is very fast, but it requires the construction of a deterministic automaton in the form of a lexicographic tree as in Figure 2.3, page 51, which is costly in space and time. In order to overcome this, Revuz proposed to replace the lexicographic tree with a pseudo-minimization [Revuz, 1991][41]. The algorithm that we are going to present on page 105 constructs the minimal deterministic automaton in a direct manner. But as we improve the space requirements we lose in speed as we are shall see in section 7.1, page 101.

5.2 Minimization of transducers

In our definition of transducers (section 3.3, page 74), we assumed that the underlying automaton was deterministic. The question of determinization therefore did not arise. On the other hand, we must now consider the problem of minimizing a transducer. A priori, this might seem to be rather simple: it suffices to consider a new kind of transition table where the outputs are taken into account. By way of example, reconsider the dictionary of page 84 to which we have added some grammatical information[42] (Figure 5.5).

```
race  V
rage  V
rice  N
```

Figure 5.5: A dictionary with three words and grammatical
information

---

[41] A dynamic version was later given in [Revuz, 2000].

[42] *V* for *verb*, *N* for *noun*, *s* for *singular*.

98

If we want to associate the information only after having recognized the word (Figure 5.6), we can only partially minimize the corresponding transducer Figure 5.7), as in the case of a multi-terminal automaton (section 2.6, page 54). On the other hand, if we allow the algorithm to output as we read the words, it is possible. (Figure 5.8). Obviously, this emission presupposes the complete recognition of the word.

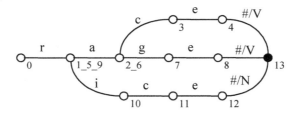

Figure 5.6: A first transducer

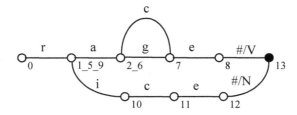

Figure 5.7: A partially minimized transducer

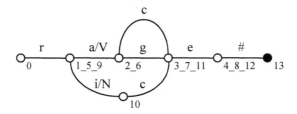

Figure 5.8: A minimal transducer for the same dictionary

The solution is therefore to shift the output as far to the left as possible, taking into account decomposing them in subsequences of letters before we apply a minimization algorithm. This idea was proposed by Mehryar Mohri [Mohri, 1994, 2000] and it can be extended to other types of transducers [Mohri, 1997][43]. The transducer thus constructed is unique (up to renumbering) and we can call it the minimal transducer associated with the initial transducer.

Thus, the transducer in Figure 5.6 has as its associated minimal transducer the one Figure 5.8. Unfortunately, it is not always the case that a minimal transducer has, as its underlying automaton, the corresponding minimal automaton (see Figure 7.10, page 155).

---

[43] See also [Béal, Carton, 2001] and [Choffrut, 2003].

5.3 Determinism and minimization

The minimization of an automaton looks at first sight like a kind of "reverse determinization". One attempts in fact to merge the states that are the goals of identical transitions.

The idea for such an algorithm is due to Janusz Brzozowski [Brzozowski, 1962ab] and it allows us to go directly from an automaton without ε-transitions (not necessarily deterministic) to a minimal deterministic automaton by applying the algorithm of determinization twice (a first time from right to left and a second time from left to right).

Let us take again the same example (Figure 4.6, page 84) and let us consider its reverse automaton (Figure 5.9). We use the character # as end-of-word character, but also as begin-of-word character.

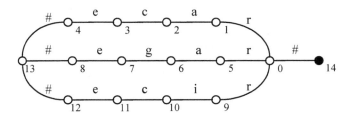

Figure 5.9: The reverse automaton

Let us construct the determinization table of the reverse automaton (Figure 5.10). We obtain a deterministic automaton (Figure 5.11).

	a	c	e	i	g	r	#
0							14
1						0	
2	1						
3		2					
4			3				
5						0	
6	5						
7					6		
8			7				
9						0	
10				9			
11		10					
12			11				
13							4, 8, 12
4_8_12			3, 7, 11				
3_7_11		2, 10			6		
2_10	1			9			

Figure 5.10: The first determinization table

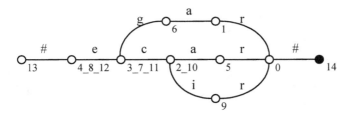

Figure 5.11: The result of the first determinization

We now reverse the automaton (Figure 5.12) and apply determinization (Figure 5.13) to finally obtain the minimal deterministic automaton (Figure 5.14).

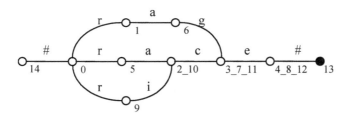

Figure 5.12: The reverse automaton of the reverse automaton

	a	c	e	i	g	r	#
0						1, 5, 9	
1	6						
5	2_10						
6					3_7_11		
9				2_10			
14							0
4_8_12							13
3_7_11			4_8_12				
2_10		3_7_11					
1_5_9	6, 2_10			2_10			
2_6_10		3_7_11			3_7_11		

Figure 5.13: The second determinization table

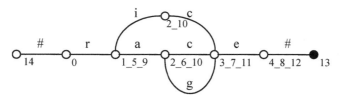

Figure 5.14: The minimal deterministic automaton

Let us observe that the automaton in Figure 5.14 is really the same as the one in Figure 5.3 (up to renumbering of states)!

5.4 Exercises

1. Go back to the resulting determinized automaton of section 4.4, page 91, and minimize it as in section 5.1.2, page 93.

2. Go back to the resulting determinized automaton of section 4.4, page 91, and minimize it as in section 5.1.4, page 97.

3. Go back to the first resulting automaton[44] of section 4.4, page 91, and minimize it as in section 5.3, page 101.

---

[44] The non deterministic automaton without ε-transition.

6. Constructing an automaton

6.1 Some definitions

Let $\mathcal{A} = (\mathcal{Q}, \mathcal{L}, q_0, q_1, \delta)$ be an automaton with final transitions (see section 3.2.4, page 70).

6.1.1 Two new types of states

A state p is called *divergent* if and only if[45] it possesses at least two outgoing transitions:

$$\exists \, \ell_1, \ell_2 \in \mathcal{L}, \ell_1 \neq \ell_2, \delta(p, \ell_1) \neq \varnothing, \delta(p, \ell_2) \neq \varnothing$$

A state p is called *convergent* if and only if it is not a terminal state and if is possesses at least two incoming transitions:

$$p \neq q_1 \text{ and } \exists \, p_1, p_2 \in \mathcal{Q}, \exists \, \ell_1, \ell_2 \in \mathcal{L}, (p_1, \ell_1) \neq (p_2, \ell_2), \delta(p_1, \ell_1) = \delta(p_2, \ell_2) = p$$

For example, our last automaton (Figure 5.14, page 105) possesses two divergent states (1_5_9 and 2_6_10) and one convergent state (3_7_11).

---

[45] In the case of an automaton with non-terminal final states, it suffices to add to the definition that these states are divergent.

6.1.2 The height and the cardinal of a state

We observed in section 4.1.3, page 47, that we can associate to each state a natural number, its *height*, which is the maximal number of transitions necessary to reach the final state. We also define the *cardinal* of a state [Revuz, 1991] as the number of sequences recognized by the sub-automaton that has this state as its initial state:

$$\forall\, p \in \mathbf{2},\ \mathrm{Cardinal}(p) = |L(\mathbf{2}', \mathcal{A}, p, q_t, \delta')|$$

This number is defined recursively by the following formula:

$$|q_t| = 1$$
$$\forall\, p \in \mathbf{2},\ |p| = \Sigma_{\{q/\exists\, \ell\, \in\, \mathcal{A}\ \text{with}\ \delta(p,\,\ell)\,=\,q\}}|q|$$

For instance, given our last automaton (Figure 5.14, page 105):

- The states 2_10, 3_7_11 and 4_8_12 have cardinal 1

- The state 2_6_10 has cardinal 2

- The state 0 and 1_5_9 have cardinal 3.

6.1.3 The construction of the minimal deterministic automaton

We will now give a detailed presentation of an algorithm for the construction of the minimal deterministic automaton based on algorithms proposed by:

- Jan Daciuk and Stoyan Mihov, for the case of a sorted list of words[46] [Daciuk, 1998], [Mihov, 1998, 1999].

- Jan Daciuk, for the case of an unsorted list of words [Daciuk, 1998].

- Dominique Revuz, for the use of the notion of the height of a state [Revuz, 2000], used for the reduction of the number of comparisons.

Other quite similar algorithms exist as well, for example[47], an algorithm proposed by Bruce W. Watson, who deploys prior sorting of the words in the list by decreasing length [Watson, 1998, 2003]. This close relation has led the authors of these papers to

---

[46] Unfortunately, this is not a classical alphabetic sorting algorithm, but a lexicographical one (i.e. based on characters). In French, for instance, a large number of rules must be taken into account in the case of a alphabetic sorting (in particular, the inter-classification of upper-case and lower-case letters, of accentuated letters, of so-called ligatures, etc. [Labonté, 1998]. It is yet more complex for sorting proper names [Tran, Maurel, Savary, 2005]!

[47] We should also cite [Holzmann, Puri, 1999] and [Ciura, Deorowicz, 1999]. We recommend [Watson, 2001] for further information.

write a synthetic presentation of their approaches [Daciuk *et al.*, 1998, 2000]. The algorithm due to Jan Daciuk has recently been extended to cyclic automata by Rafael C. Carrasco and Mikel L. Forcada [Carrasco, Forcada, 2002].

We shall show how to adapt these approaches to our methods of representation. We will make use here, in order to reduce the number of states that need to be compared, of the notion of a cardinal and the number of following transitions. Indeed, the equality of these three numbers is a necessary (but not sufficient!) condition for merging states. The calculation of the cardinal is used above all to construct the hash transducers that will be presented in section 7.2, page 158.

6.2 Construction on the basis of a list of sorted words

Let us consider the following example: we want to construct the minimal deterministic automaton that recognizes the dictionary in Figure 6.1. This list does not contain any duplicates, which we can eliminate as we sort the list[48].

---

[48] If this were not the case, it would suffice to decrement the cardinals when encountering duplicates, see section 6.3.5, page 144 and section 8.2.4, page 182.

```
rack
rank
reek
reeks
rick
rink
seek
```

Figure 6.1: A dictionary of seven words

6.2.1 The first word

We initialize the automaton with the first word, *rack* (Figure 6.2), and then we construct a table with four columns. The table HCLG (*Height, Cardinal, Label, Goal*), Figure 6.3, represents our first word. The heights are decreasing beginning with 5 (length of the word plus one characters for the end of the word) and the cardinals are all set to 1.

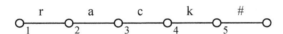

Figure 6.2: The first automaton

	Height	Cardinal	Label	Goal
1	5	1	r	2
2	4	1	a	3
3	3	1	c	4
4	2	1	k	5
5	1	1	#	0

Figure 6.3: The first HCLG table

6.2.2 Adding a word

We start by reading the beginning of the second word (*rank*) from the table above (here, line 1 and line 2) by incrementing the *Cardinal* and by calculating the new height of the state (the maximum of the height of the previous word and the length of the word that remains to be written – here the two words have the same length, the heights remain the same).

We then copy line 3 at the end of the table (line 6 in Figure 6.4) in order to have room to add the transition labeled *n* (line 7). At line 6, we calculate the new height of the state (here, it remains equal to 3) and the new cardinal of the state (here, 2).

In order to indicate that the lines 6 and 7 represent the same state, we will put the value 0 in the column *Height* in line 7. In this line, we take advantage of the column *Cardinal* and insert the number of following transitions for this state (here, 2).

To indicate the deletion of line 3, we erase its *Height* and its *Cardinal*. The goal *But* in line 2 is now 6.

We continue with our second word (lines 8 and 9) and obtain the automaton given in Figure 6.5.

Finally, we already anticipate the following word, *reek*, which has just one letter, as a common prefix with *rank*, the letter *r*. We add one letter to this prefix (*ra*) and store the states we have used to recognize the end of the word (*nk#*): 6_7[49]/8/9, in bold face in Figure 6.4 and in black[50] in Figure 6.5.

---

[49] As we number the transitions and not the states, 6_7 designates the source of the transitions 6 and 7.

[50] Here the states in black are thus not final states, in contrast to the figures in the first chapters. The final states are those that are those reached by the final transitions, labeled with the character #.

		Height	Cardinal	Label	Goal
Previous automaton	1	5→5	1→2	r	2
	2	4→4	1→2	a	3→6
	3	3→0	1→0	c	4
	4	2	1	k	5
	5	1	1	#	0
Copied State	6	3→3	1→2	c	4
	7	0	2	**n**	8
New states	8	2	1	**k**	9
	9	1	1	**#**	0

Figure 6.4: The HCLG table after the addition of the second word

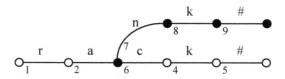

Figure 6.5: The automaton after the addition of the second word

6.2.3 Partial minimization

Since we have stored the lines that we have used, we can now begin the minimization by rereading, beginning at the end, in the automaton the word we have just added. This rereading will not go to the end of the word, but only with respect to the states stored so far.

We therefore start from line 9 (*the current state* of the minimization). In principle, minimization proceeds in four steps:

1. The look-up of a state with the same height, cardinal and number of following transitions as the current state.

If a state is found, we move on to step 2.

2. The comparison of the transitions of the current state with those of the state found at step 1.

If the two state are the same, we can merge them and pass on to step 3, if not we return to step 1 for a new look-up, as there can be several states satisfying the same search criteria.

3. The substitution of the goal of the transition that arrives at the current state with the number of the state found at step 1. This transition was stored during the addition of the word.

4. The deletion of the lines corresponding to the current state.

Let us spell out step 1 (Figure 6.6):

- We read the height and the cardinal on line 9: 1 and 1.

- Look-up in the previous automaton of a state with the same height and cardinal, with a single following transition, line 5.

We move on to step 2:

- Comparison of the labels and the goals of the two states (9 and 5): they are the same.

Step 3:

- Substitution of *Goal* in line 8 by the number of the line found: 5.

And step 4:

- Removal of line 9.

We restart with line 8, which is found to be the same as line 4: same steps as above.

We reuse step 1 with line 6 by looking for a state with height 3 in the table, which is not the case. We have now minimized the part we have selected to obtain what Mihov [Mihov, 1998] calls a minimal deterministic automaton *except for one word* (Figure 6.7). It turns out that the automaton we now have is minimal, but this is not always the case, as we shall see in section 6.2.4.

	Height	Cardinal	Label	Goal
1	5	2	r	2
2	4	2	a	6
3	0	0	c	4
4	2	1	k	5
5	1	1	#	0
6	3	2	c	4
7	0	2	n	8→4
8	2	1	k	9→5
9	1	1	#	0

Previous automaton: rows 1–5
Copied state: rows 6, 7
New states: rows 8, 9

Figure 6.6: The HCLG table after minimization

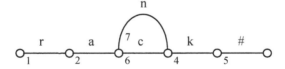

Figure 6.7: An automaton that is minimal except for one word

6.2.4 The encounter with a convergent state

If, instead of the word *reek*, the third word of our dictionary, we wanted to first add (respecting alphabetic order) the word *rant*, what we have just done would not apply: in adding this word in the automaton in Figure 6.7, the new automaton would also recognize *ract* (Figure 6.8) which we obviously do not want to recognize!

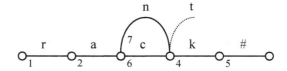

Figure 6.8: Impossible to restart from state 4

It is here that the look-up of the common prefix of *rank* and the following word in the dictionary comes in. When we add a letter to this prefix, we have *ra* if the following word is *reek* and *rank* if it is *rant*. With respect to the latter, minimization (which is only partial) affects only line 9, as in Figure 6.9.

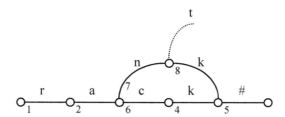

Figure 6.9: A minimal automaton except one word that is not minimal

118

6.2.5 Adding a third word

Let us consider the real third word in the dictionary (*reek*). We read only the first line (the *r*) by computing the new height and the new cardinal to come to line 2 which we copy in lines 8_9 (Figure 6.10). With respect to this line we compute the new height (4) and the new cardinal. In line 9, we put 0 in the column *Height*, 2 in the column *Cardinal* (number of output transitions) and 10 in the column *Goal*. We remove *Height* and *Cardinal* in line 2.

We then add the lines 11 and 12 to obtain the automaton in Figure 6.11. Since the word *reek* is a prefix of the following word, *reeks*, there is no minimization[51], because it would have to start after *reek#* (common prefix plus one letter).

---

[51] In Figure 6.11, we can merge the terminal states, but this can already be seen in table HCLG in Figure 6.10 where the goals of lines 5 and 12 are equal to 0.

		Height	Cardinal	Label	Goal
	1	5→5	2→3	r	2→8
	2	4→0	2→0	a	6
	3	0	0	c	4
Previous automaton	4	2	1	k	5
	5	1	1	#	0
	6	3	2	c	4
	7	0	2	n	4
Copied state	8	4→4	2→3	a	6
	9	0	2	e	10
	10	3	1	e	11
New states	11	2	1	k	12
	12	1	1	#	0

Figure 6.10: The third HCLG table

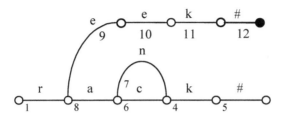

Figure 6.11: The third automaton

6.2.6 Adding a partially written word

Let us now add the word *reeks*. We read the lines 1, 9, 10 and 11 by changing *Height* (which this time increases by 1, as *reeks* has one more letter than the previous words) and *Cardinal* (Figure 6.12). We copy line 12 to the end of the table and add the transition labeled *s* (lines 13 and 14).

The *Height* of line 14 is set to 0 and the *Cardinal* to *2* (the number of following transitions). Finally, we modify the *Goal* of line 11 (12 becomes 13) and we mark that line 12 is to be deleted by setting *Height* and *Cardinal* to 0. We need only to add line 15 (Figure 6.13).

Since the common prefix with the following word, *rick*, has only one letter, we store the path 10/11/13_14/15 (*eks#*).

Minimization begins with line 15: we look for a height 1 and a cardinal 1, for the next transition, we find line 5, compare the labels and the goals, then we merge the states (that is, we remove line 15 and write 5 into *Goal* of line 14). Then we treat line 13: we look for a height 2 and a cardinal 2, which are not found in any line. We obtain our fourth automaton (Figure 6.14).

		Height	Cardinal	Label	Goal
	1	5→6	3→4	r	8
	2	0	0	a	6
	3	0	0	c	4
	4	2	1	k	5
	5	1	1	#	0
Previous automaton	6	3	2	c	4
	7	0	2	n	4
	8	4→5	3→4	a	6
	9	0	2	e	10
	10	3→4	1→2	**e**	11
	11	2→3	1→2	**k**	12→13
	12	1→0	1→0	#	0
Copied state	**13**	1→2	1→2	#	0
	14	0	2	**s**	15→5
New state	**15**	1	1	#	0

Figure 6.12: The fourth HCLG table

123

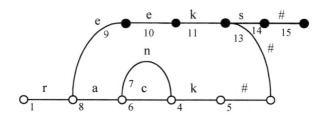

Figure 6.13: The automaton after the addition of the fourth word

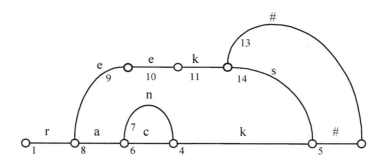

Figure 6.14: The fourth automaton

6.2.7 Adding a third transition to a state

Until now, all our states had only one or two outgoing transitions. The addition of the word *rick* will provide a different example.

We read the beginning of the word (the *r*) and adjust the columns *Height* and *Cardinal*, and then we copy and complete the state 8_9 beginning at line 15 (Figure 6.15). In Lines 16 and 17, *Height* is set to 0 and *Cardinal* to 3 (the number of following transitions[52]). The *Goal* of line 1 becomes *15*. Then we add the lines 18 to 20.

The common prefix of the word *rick* and the following word in the dictionary, *rink*, augmented with one letter is *ric*. We therefore store the path 19/20 (*k#*, Figure 6.16).

Minimization now consists in merging the states 5 and 20 and then 4 and 19 (Figure 6.17).

		Height	Cardinal	Label	Goal
	1	6→6	4→5	r	8→15
	2	0	0		6
	3		0	c	4
	4	2	1	k	5
	5	1	1	#	0
Previous automaton	6	3	2	c	4
	7	0	2	n	4
	8	5→0	4→0	a	6
	9	0	2→0	e	10
	10	4	2	e	11
	11	3	2	k	13
	12	0	0	#	0
	13	2	2	#	0
	14	0	2	s	5
Copied state	15	5→5	4→5	a	6
	16	0	2→3	e	10
	17	0	3	i	18
New states	18	3	1	c	19→4
	19	2	1	**k**	20→5
	20	1	1	#	0

Figure 6.15: The fifth HCLG table

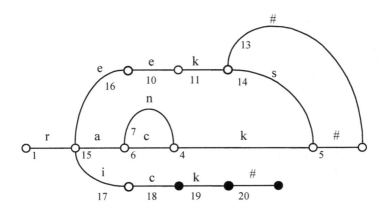

Figure 6.16: The automaton after the addition of the fifth word

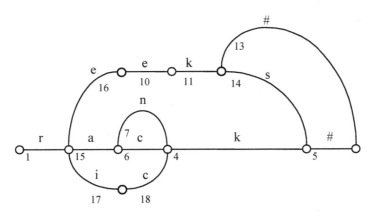

Figure 6.17: The fifth automaton

6.2.8 Merging divergent states

The beginning of the following word, *rink*, is read on lines 1 and 17. Line 18 is copied, lines 19 and 20, to create, line 20, a transition labeled with the letter *n*. We finish with the lines 21 and 22 (Figure 6.18 and Figure 6.19).

The common prefix of the last two words in the dictionary, *rink* and *seek*, plus one letter is therefore *r*. We mark this path with *ink#*: 15_16_17/19_20/21/22. The start of the minimization merges the states 22 and 5, then the states 21 and 4 (Figure 6.18 and Figure 6.20).

Let us now consider the minimization of state 19_20: we look for a state with *Height* 3 and *Cardinal* 2, containing the same two following transitions that can be found in line 6. We then compare the labels and the goals of the two transitions of each state (lines 19 and 6, then lines 20 and 7). As these are the same, we remove the lines 19 and 20 and put 6 as *Goal* in line 17. We then look for a state with *Height* 5, which is nonexistent; we now have our sixth automaton.

		Height	Cardinal	Label	Goal
	1	6→6	5→6	r	15
	2	0	0	a	6
	3	0	0	c	4
	4	2	1	k	5
	5	1	1	#	0
	6	3	2	c	4
	7	0	2	n	4
	8	0	0	a	6
Previous	9	0	0	e	10
automaton	10	4	2	e	11
	11	3	2	k	13
	12	0	0	#	0
	13	2	2	#	0
	14	0	2	s	5
	15	5→5	5→6	a	6
	16	0	3	e	10
	17	0	3	**i**	18→19→6
	18	3→0	1→0	c	4
Copied	**19**	3→3	1→2	c	4
state	**20**	0	2	**n**	21→4
New states	**21**	2	1	**k**	22→5
	22	1	1	#	0

Figure 6.18: The sixth HCLG table

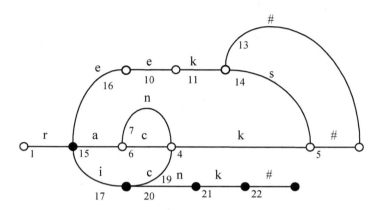

Figure 6.19: The automaton after the addition of the sixth word

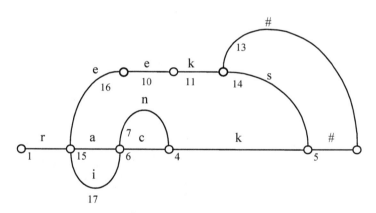

Figure 6.20: The sixth automaton

6.2.9 Adding a word beginning with another letter

We now consider adding the word *seek*, the last word in our list. A priori, there is no problem, state 1 is copied to line 19 (Figure 6.21); it suffices to observe that the reading of the table begins with this line: For this, we put 19 on line 0 of the HCLG table[53]. As this word is the last, minimization concerns the entire path: 21/22/23/24 (Figure 6.22).

Minimization stops in line 22, because none of the states with *Height 3* has *Cardinal* 1. The minimal deterministic automaton that recognizes our dictionary on page 111 is thus the one shown in Figure 6.23.

---

[53] An other solution is to use a begin-of-word character, as in section 5.3 page 101.

		Height	Cardinal	Label	Goal
Beginning of the table	0				19
Previous automaton	1	6→0	6→0	r	15
	2	0	0	a	6
	3	0	0	c	4
	4	2	1	k	5
	5	1	1	#	0
	6	3	2	c	4
	7	0	2	n	4
	8	0	0	a	6
	9	0	0	e	10
	10	4	2	e	11
	11	3	2	k	13
	12	0	0	#	0
	13	2	2	#	0
	14	0	2	s	5
	15	5	6	a	6
	16	0	3	e	10
	17	0	3	i	6
	18	0	0	c	4
State copied	19	6→6	6→7	r	15
	20	0	2	s	21
New states	21	4	1	e	22
	22	3	1	e	23→4
	23	2	1	k	24→5
	24	1	1	#	0

Figure 6.21: The final HCLG table

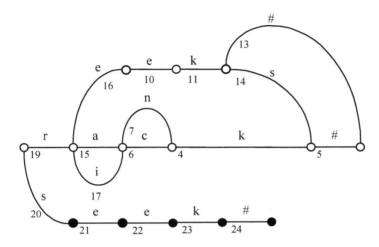

Figure 6.22: The automaton after the addition of the seventh word

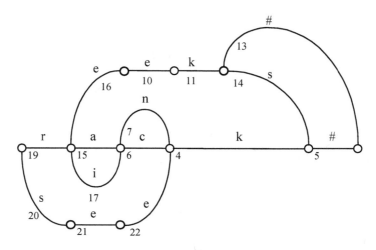

Figure 6.23: The final automaton

6.3 Construction on the basis of an unsorted list

What will change in the case that the list is assumed to be unsorted?

1. First of all, it is clearly useless to compare a word with the word that succeeds it in the list, since the latter can be any word in the dictionary. Minimization will therefore take place in a complete manner at each stage, at the risk of undoing what was done at an earlier stage.

2. In addition, we must take into account encountering a convergent state (the case described in section 6.2.4, page 118, is now a real possibility).

3.   Finally, since our list is not sorted, it may also contain duplicates.

Let us consider again our previous list, but we assume that the first four words are *rink*, *rank*, *rick* and *rack* and that the word *rink* occurs twice (Figure 6.24).

```
rink
rank
rick
rack
rink
reek
reeks
seek
```

Figure 6.24: A list of eight words (unsorted and with a duplicate)

6.3.1 Storing convergent states

Since the occurrence of a convergent state will require special treatment (see section 6.2.4, page 118), we will need to add another column to our table, the column *Before*. This column will only contain the number 1, except for the first line. The table obtained after reading the first word, *rink*, is in Figure 6.25 and the corresponding automaton in Figure 6.26.

	Height	Cardinal	Before	Label	Goal
1	5	1	0	r	2
2	4	1	1	i	3
3	3	1	1	n	4
4	2	1	1	k	5
5	1	1	1	#	0

Figure 6.25: The first HCBLG table

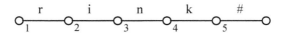

Figure 6.26: The first automaton

6.3.2 A complete minimization at each stage

When we introduce the second word, *rank*, we construct the table in the same manner as in section 6.2, page 110, with the exception of the copy, where the transitions are sorted alphabetically (the *i* of line 2 can be found in line 7 and the *a* of the second word in 6). As we will not use the column *Before* of line 7, we set it to 0 (Figure 6.27). When we minimize, we need to add a step to deal with this new column: we decrement the number of entering transitions of the goals of the deleted lines and, at the same time, we increment the number of entering transitions in the state resulting from merging.

With respect to our example, when we merge lines 10 and 5, the value *Before* of line 5 goes from 1 to 2, without any other modification, because the goal of line 10 is the final state. On the other hand, the merge of lines 9 and 4 now involves two actions: the column *Before* increases from 1 to 2 on line 4 and from *2* to 1 on line 5. Finally, the merging of lines 8 and 3 again modifies the column *Before* which goes from 1 to 2 on line 3 and from 2 to 1 on line 4. We thus obtain the minimal deterministic automation in Figure 6.28.

		Height	Cardinal	Before	Label	Goal
	1	5	2	0	**r**	6
	2	0	0	1	i	3
Previous automaton	3	3	1	1→2	n	4
	4	2	1	1→2→1	k	5
	5	1	1	1→2→1	#	0
State copied	**6**	4	2	1	**a**	8→3
	7	0	2	0	i	3
	8	3	1	1	**n**	9→4
New states	**9**	2	1	1	**k**	10→5
	10	1	1	1	**#**	0

Figure 6.27: The second HCBLG table

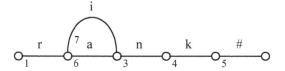

Figure 6.28: The second automaton

6.3.3 Dealing with a convergent state

Let us deal with the third word (*rick*). After reading the transition labeled *r* (line 1) and *i* (line 7), we arrive in state 3 which is convergent (we have a 2 in the column *Before*). We cannot add, as we already remarked in section 6.2.4, page 118, a transition labeled with *c* (Figure 6.29), because the automaton would also recognize *rack* which we do not wish to recognize at this stage of the construction (we want to recognize for the moment only three words and not four).

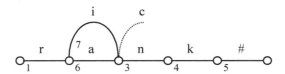

Figure 6.29: Impossible to restart from state 3

We will therefore duplicate state 3 by copying line 3 in order to add to the corresponding state the transition labeled with *c*, in alphabetical order (lines 8 and 9 in Figure 6.30). Since we want to duplicate, we will not remove line 3 and we will not change the *Goal* of line 6. State 3 loses an incoming transition (column *Before*, 2 becomes 1), and is no longer converged. On the other hand, state 4 now is convergent (it is *Goal* in lines 3 and 9): line 8, column *Before*, 1 becomes 2.

We then add lines 10 and 11 and obtain the automaton in Figure 6.31. We store the path corresponding to the entire: 1/7/8/10/11. From now on nothing new: lines 10 and 11 disappear, being merged respectively with lines 5 and 4; we increment the column

139

Before in line 4 which goes from 2 to 3. We thus have the minimal deterministic automaton (Figure 6.32). Let us remark that like Penelope, we needed to undo some of the work performed previously, something that does not happen if the list sorted.

		Height	Cardinal	Before	Label	Goal
	1	5	3	0	r	6
	2	0	0	1	i	3
	3	3	1	2→1	n	4
Previous automaton	4	2	1	1→2→3	k	5
	5	1	1	1→2→1	#	0
	6	4	3	1	a	3
	7	0	2	0	i	8
Copied state	8	3	2	1	c	10→4
	9	0	2	0	n	4
New state	10	2	1	1	k	11→5
	11	1	1	1	#	0

Figure 6.30: The third HCBLG table

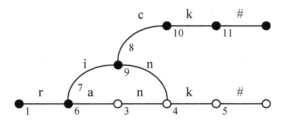

Figure 6.31 The automaton after the addition of the third word

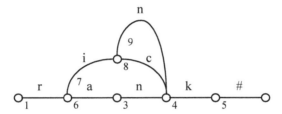

Figure 6.32: The third automaton

6.3.4 The minimization of the duplicated state

Let us now add the word *rack*. When we come to line 3 (Figure 6.33), we check whether this state is convergent or not in order to find out if we need to duplicate this state (in case it is convergent) or to copy it (in case it is not). As it is not convergent (1 in the column *Before*), we copy line 3 to the end of the table and add, in lexicographic order, the transition labeled *c* (lines 10 and 11). Now we only need to add lines 12 and 13 and to store the path 1/6/10/12/13.

Minimization begins with merging lines 13 and 5 (line 5 is incremented in *Before*). Then we take care of lines 12 and 4 (line 5 is decremented in *Before*, whereas line 4 is incremented). When we merge state 10_11 with state 8_9, line 8 goes from 1 to 2 in *Before*, and as we are merging two transitions leading to state 4, the number of transitions coming to this state is therefore reduced by 2 (4 becomes 2). Minimization is finished (Figure 6.34).

		Height	Cardinal	Before	Label	Goal
	1	5	4	0	**r**	6
	2	0	0	1	i	3
	3	0	0	1	n	4
Previous automaton	4	2	1	3→4→2	k	5
	5	1	1	1→2→1	#	0
	6	4	4	1	**a**	10→8
	7	0	2	0	i	8
	8	3	2	1→2	c	4
	9	0	2	0	n	4
Copied state	**10**	0	2	1	**c**	12→4
	11	3	2		n	4
New state	**12**	2	1	1	**k**	13→5
	13	1	1		#	0

Figure 6.33: The fourth HCBLG table

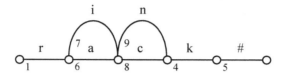

Figure 6.34: The fourth automaton

6.3.5 Adding a word that is already recognized

The fifth word, by chance or by error, is already represented in the automaton. If we apply our algorithm:

- The cardinals are incremented

- The heights don't change

- Convergent states are duplicated

it is easy to decrement the cardinals when we see that the automaton already recognizes the word. On the other hand, it is more complex to delete duplicated states.

In order to avoid this, and taking into account duplicates, the easiest solutions is to read the words into the automaton a first time without modifying anything and without checking if a state is convergent or not. If we come to a final transition at the end of the word, we notice the word is already contained in the automaton and we move on to the next word. If not, we start the construction algorithm.

6.4 Exercises

1. Construct the minimal deterministic automaton that recognizes the dictionary in Figure 6.35, as in section 6.2, page 110.

2. Same question with the unsorted list in Figure 6.36, as in section 6.3, page 134.

```
code
compose
decode
decompose
defuse
demerge
fuse
merge
recode
recompose
refuse
remerge
```

Figure 6.35: A sorted dictionary of English verbs

code
decode
recode
compose
decompose
recompose
fuse
defuse
refuse
merge
demerge
remerge

Figure 6.36: An unsorted list of English verbs

7. Constructing a transducer

7.1 Constructing a p-sub-sequential transducer

We will now turn our attention to the problem of constructing a transducer [Mihov, Maurel, 2000]. We use the same series of examples again, and start by associating with each word a morphosyntactic code[54] (Figure 7.1).

```
rack  V
rank  A
reek  Ns
reeks Np
rick  V
rink  Ns
seek  V
```

Figure 7.1: A dictionary consisting of seven words
and their morphosyntactic codes

To construct a transducer, it suffices to add a column *Output* to the HCLG table, where we are going to store the leftmost outputs, which are then concatenated in order to obtain the final output.

---

[54] *V* for *verb*, *A* for *adjective*, *N* for *noun*, *s* for *singular*, *p* for *plural*.

7.1.1 The goal of the construction

The construction is identical to the one we used to construct an automaton. All we need to do is to put the output on the first line (Figure 7.2 and Figure 7.3).

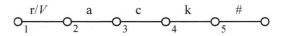

Figure 7.2: The first transducer

	Height	Cardinal	Label	Goal	Output
1	5	1	r	2	V
2	4	1	a	3	
3	3	1	c	4	
4	2	1	k	5	
5	1	1	#	0	

Figure 7.3: The first HCLGO table

7.1.2 Moving the outputs to the right

For the second entry, *rank* →*A*, we shift the output to the state just copied (lines 6 and 7).

As long as we do not try to merge the lines containing the same *Output* value, the construction of a transducer is identical to that of the underlying automaton.

This is the case here (Figure 5.6, page 62): the merge does not affect lines 6 and 7, but only lines 8 and 9 (Figure 7.4 and Figure 7.5).

	Height	Cardinal	Label	Goal	Output
1	5	2	r	2	
2	4	2	a	6	
3	0	0	c	4	
4	2	1	k	5	
5	1	1	#	0	
6	3	2	c	4	V
7	0	2	n	4	A
8	2	1	k	5	
9	1	1	#	0	

Figure 7.4: The second HCLGO table

149

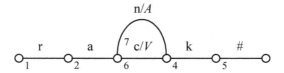

Figure 7.5: The second transducer

The same applies to the next word (Figure 7.6).

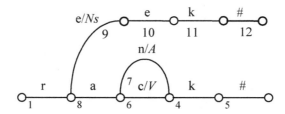

Figure 7.6: The third transducer

7.1.3 The common prefix of two output strings

For the fourth entry, *reeks* → *Np*, we read the automaton until line 9 where the only output is *Ns*. The output of the fourth word and that of line 9 both begin with the letters *N*. We then split the strings into their common prefix (*N*) on line 9 (Figure 7.7) and two specific output strings (*s* and *p*) on the lines 13 and 14, respectively.

Figure 7.8 shows the resulting transducer, before adding the fifth entry, *rick* → *V*.

	Height	Cardinal	Label	Goal	Output
1	6	4	r	8	
2	0	0	a	6	
3	0	0	c	4	
4	2	1	k	5	
5	1	1	#	0	
6	3	2	c	4	V
7	0	2	n	4	A
8	5	4	a	6	
9	0	2	e	10	N
10	4	2	e	11	
11	3	2	k	12→13	
12	0	0	#	0	
13	2	2	#	0	s
14	0	2	s	5	p
15	1	1	#	0	

Figure 7.7: The fourth HCLGO table

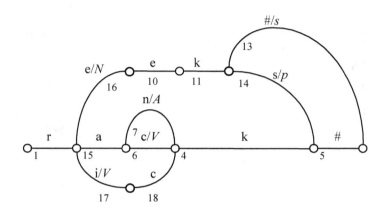

Figure 7.8: The fifth transducer

7.1.4 Minimizing the transducer

Adding the sixth entry, *rink* → *Ns*, illustrates the small difference between the two algorithms (automaton *versus* transducer): it suffices, for every transition, to include *Output* when comparing *Label* and *Goal*.

When we construct the sixth transducer, the Output of line 17, *V*, must be shifted to line 18 (Figure 7.9), whereas the new output, *Ns*, is moved to line 20.

The goal of the minimization is the same for an automaton and a transducer (see Figure 5.18, page 72). However, after having deleting lines 21 and 22, we realize that the states 19_20 and 6_7 share the same values for the columns *Height, Cardinal, Label* and *Goal*, but not in the *Output* column, which prevents the continuation of the minimization. We therefore have to stop, having obtained the transducer in Figure 7.10. Its underlying automaton is not the automaton in Figure 5.20, page 73.

	Height	Cardinal	Label	Goal	Output
1	6	6	r	15	
2	0	0	a	6	
3	0	0	c	4	
4	2	1	k	5	
5	1	1	#	0	
6	3	2	c	4	V
7	0	2	n	4	A
8	0	0	a	6	
9	0	0	e	10	N
10	4	2	e	11	
11	3	2	k	13	
12	0	0	#	0	
13	2	2	#	0	s
14	0	2	s	5	p
15	5	6	a	6	
16	0	3	e	10	N
17	0	3	i	19	
18	0	0	c	4	
19	3	2	c	4	V
20	0	2	n	4	Ns
21	2	1	k	5	
22	1	1	#	0	

Figure 7.9: The sixth HCLGO table

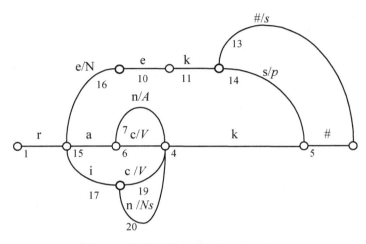

Figure 7.10: The sixth transducer

7.1.5 The last word

When adding the final entry, *seek* → *V*, minimizing the transducer consists of deleting the last two lines of the table of Figure 7.11. The transducer in Figure 7.12 is minimal.

	Height	Cardinal	Label	Goal	Output
0				21	
1	0	0	r	15	
2	0	0	a	6	
3	0	0	c	4	
4	2	1	k	5	
5	1	1	#	0	
6	3	2	c	4	V
7	0	2	n	4	A
8	0	0	a	6	
9	0	0	e	10	N
10	4	2	e	11	
11	3	2	k	13	
12	0	0	#	0	
13	2	2	#	0	s
14	0	2	s	5	p
15	5	6	a	6	
16	0	3	e	10	N
17	0	3	i	19	
18	0	0	c	4	
19	3	2	c	4	V
20	0	2	n	4	Ns
21	6	7	r	15	
22	0	2	s	21	V
23	4	1	e	24	
24	3	1	e	4	
25	2	1	k	5	
26	1	1	#	0	

Figure 7.11: The final HCLGO table

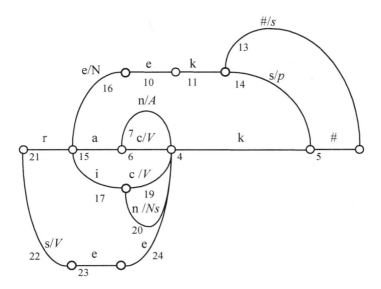

Figure 7.12: The final transducer

7.1.6 Adding a homograph

As we observed in section 6.2, page 110, our dictionary is sorted alphabetically: if, by chance, the list contains duplicates, they are eliminated when sorting. When constructing a transducer, however, the same word might appear more than once with different output strings (of the homographs). In order to avoid reading a homograph of a word already written in the transducer, we are going to make use of the sorting to factorize the output strings.

For example: let us add the entry *rank* → *Ns* to our dictionary of page 147. When sorting, we replace the two lines *rank* → *A* and *rank* → *Ns* with a single line, *rank* → *A|Ns* (this is called a p-sequential output). The algorithm stays the same, except for comparing the output strings:

- A p-sequential output (or one of its suffixes) will necessarily be shifted to the right and it is thus found again after the last divergent state we came across.

- A prefix of a p-sequential output is a common prefix of all its sub strings. With respect to the example with the word *rank*, no prefixes are now possible.

7.2   Construction of a hash transducer

7.2.1 Lexicographical sorting

A particular type of transducer is the hash transducer [Revuz, 1991], which consists in associating each word with its position in the lexicographical order. A particular type of transducer is the hash transducer [Revuz, 1991], which consists in associating each word with its position in the lexicographical order. This idea has been independently proposed by [Lucchesi, Kowaltowski, 1993].

In fact, the construction is carried out in two steps:

1.   constructing and minimizing the underlying automaton

2.   then by filling in the column *Output* in all lines.

Suppose that the Cardinal of the terminal state (*0* in the *Goal* column) is 1 and that the final transitions are always placed on the first position of the list of transitions following a state[55]. Then, the algorithm of filling in the column *Output* consists in:

- Putting 0 in the column *Output* of the first transition of a state.

- Calculating for all following transitions, if they exist, the sum of the output of all previous transitions and the Cardinal of the state reached by this transition.

We put 0 in the column *Output* of all non-divergent states. For the divergent states, see Figure 7.13.

---

[55] This is not exactly correct if one sorts on characters; for example, consider the character ordering used by Windows: the character # precedes the blank, the question mark and the apostrophe. Therefore, if our dictionary comprises multi-word words containing blanks, the corresponding transitions come before the final transitions.

Final transition	First non-final transition	Second non-final transition	Following transitions (non final)
Without final transition	0	Cardinal of the state reached by the first transition	Cardinal of the state reached by the previous non-final transition + the sum of its previous output
0	1	Cardinal of the state reached by the first non-final transition + 1	

Figure 7.13: Output of transitions following a divergent state

The output obtained by reading this transducer is not the concatenation, but the sum of output strings of each transition visited.

7.2.2 Example

Starting from our dictionary on Figure 6.1 page 111 and the HCLG table of Figure 6.21 page 132, we obtain the HCLGO table of Figure 7.14 and the hash transducer (Figure 7.15):

- The *Output* of line 7 is the *Cardinal* of *Goal* (4) of line 6, i.e. *1*.

- The *Output* of line 14 is the *Cardinal* of *Goal* (0) of line 13, i.e. *1*.

- The *Output* of line 16 is the *Cardinal* of *Goal* (6) of line 15, i.e. *2*.

- The *Output* of line 17 is identical to the sum of the *Output* (2) of line 16 and the *Cardinal* of *Goal* (10) of line 16, *2*, i.e. the sum 2+2=4.

- The *Output* of line 20 is the *Cardinal* of *Goal* (15) of line 19, i.e. 6.

	Height	Cardinal	Label	Goal	Output
0				19	
1	0	0	r	15	
2	0	0	a	6	
3	0	0	c	4	
4	2	1	k	5	0
5	1	1	#	0	0
6	3	2	c	4	0
7	0	2	n	4	1
8	0	0	a	6	
9	0	0	e	10	
10	4	2	e	11	0
11	3	2	k	13	0
12	0	0	#	0	
13	2	2	#	0	0
14	0	2	s	5	1
15	5	6	a	6	0
16	0	3	e	10	2
17	0	3	i	6	4
18	0	0	c	4	
19	6	7	r	15	0
20	0	2	s	21	6
21	4	1	e	22	0
22	3	1	e	4	0

Figure 7.14: The hash HCLGO table

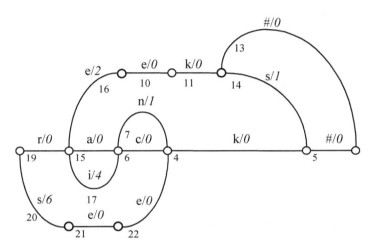

Figure 7.15: The hash transducer

7.2.3 Recognition and classification

While reading (in depth) the words recognized by the transducer, we obtain as output:

- r (line 19, output 0) a (line 15, output 0) c (line 6, output 0) k (line 4, output 0) # (line 5, output 0): the word *rack* of order 0+0+0+0+0=0

- r (line 19, output 0) a (line 15, output 0) n (line 7, output 1) k (line 4, output 0) # (line 5, output 0): the word *rank* of order 0+0+1+0+0=1

- r (line 19, output 0) e (line 16, output 2) e (line 10, output 0) k (line 11, output 0) # (line 13, output 0): the word *reek* of order 0+2+0+0+0=2

- r (line 19, output 0) e (line 16, output 2) e (line 10, output 0) k (line 11, output 0) s (line 14, output 1) # (line 5, output 0): the word *reeks* of order 0+2+0+0+1+0=3

- r (line 19, output 0) i (line 17, output 4) c (line 6, output 0) k (line 4, output 0) # (line 5, output 0): the word *rick* of order 0+4+0+0+0=4

- r (line 19, output 0) i (line 17, output 4) n (line 7, output 1) k (line 4, output 0) # (line 5, output 0): the word *rick* of order 0+4+1+0+0=5

- s (line 20, output 6) e (line 21, output 0) e (line 22, output 0) k (line 4, output 0) # (line 5, output 0): the word *seek* of order 6+0+0+0+0=6

i.e. the lexicographical order.

7.2.4 *Algorithm*

```
/* Creating an automaton on the basis of a dictionary */
Construct_automaton
{
/* Reading the first two words */
      Open_dictionary_file
      Creating_the_automaton_with_the_first_word
      next←Read_one_word_from_the_dictionary

/* Reading the next words */
      DO
      {
            current←next
            next←Read_one_word_from_the_dictionary
            Read_the_automaton
            Complete_the_automaton
#IF CONSTRUCTING_A_TRANSDUCER
            Insert_output_of_current_word
#ENDIF
            Prefix_plus_one←Calculate_end_of_the_minimisation
            Minimise_automaton_until_Prefix_plus_one
      }
      WHILE(next_word_exists)
      Close_dictionary_file
#IF CONSTRUCTING_A_HASH_TRANSDUCER
      Calculate_hash_output_strings
#ENDIF
/* Automaton created. */
}
```

7.3 Exercise

Go back to the resulting determinized minimal automaton of section 6.4, page 145, and build the hash transducer, as in section 7.2.2, page 160.

8. Additional topics

8.1 Size and Time

8.1.1 Introduction

In this chapter, we will try to estimate in an approximate manner the size and the time necessary for the construction of the minimal deterministic automaton corresponding to a list of words.

We will consider the size of the words concerned, the size of our dictionary or of our automaton, the size of the alphabet and we will substitute certain values by the maximal values that one might reach in the worst case.

8.1.2 The dictionary

We begin with the dictionary: let us assume that the dictionary contains D characters[56] and W words.

If we use a space s to store one letter and if we read this letter in time t, we will require space of size $s \times D$ for the complete dictionary and we will use $t \times D$ units of time to read it completely. In both cases, we see that the space used and the time

---

[56] Here and in what follows, we include in these values the end of word character as well.

consumed correspond to a constant value (s or t) multiplied by D. As the values taken by s or t depend on the machines and the operating systems used, it is only the data which is of interest in our evaluation; we thus assume that the size used and the time necessary for reading the data are proportional to D, which we will designate by $O(D)$.

Let w be the size of a word we wish to read from this dictionary; if this word is the last word in the list (in the worst case), we have to perform W comparisons on a word-by-word basis. If the comparison fails on the last letter of the word, we will have to make w letter-by-letter comparisons. It follows that we will at most take time $O(W{\times}w)$ to read a given word.

8.1.3 The automaton

If we construct a non-deterministic lexicographic tree from this dictionary, the number of states of this automaton is identical to the number of characters stored, plus one. The determinization of such an automaton can therefore only lead to a reduction of the number of states[57], but this reduction cannot be predicted, since it depends on the dictionaries we deploy. Thus, in the worst case, the space used by a deterministic lexicographic tree is $O(D)$. When we minimize, we reduce the number of states, that is, the size of the automaton, but we cannot estimate the new size of the automaton

---

[57] To see this, we can compare Figure 2.2, page 48 with Figure 2.3, page 51, with the Figure 4.15, page 90, and the Figure 4.17, page 91.

on the basis of the size of the dictionary. However, if **S** is the number of states of our automaton, its size will be $\mathcal{O}(\mathsf{S})$ and the complete reading of all of the words that it recognized will take time $\mathcal{O}(\mathsf{S})$.

Let **A** be the size of our alphabet, that is, the number of different possible transitions; at each state, we compare the current letter with the labels of the output transitions of this state; in the worst case, we will have **A** comparisons to make. The reading of a word will therefore take time $\mathcal{O}(\mathsf{A} \times \mathsf{w})$.

As we can see from Figure 8.1, the representation of a dictionary by a minimal deterministic automaton always represents a reduction in time and space, since in general we have **D** > **S** and **W** > **A**.

	Dictionary	Automaton
Space occupied in memory	$\mathcal{O}(\mathsf{D})$	$\mathcal{O}(\mathsf{S})$
Time to read all the words	$\mathcal{O}(\mathsf{D})$	$\mathcal{O}(\mathsf{S})$
Time to read a given word	$\mathcal{O}(\mathsf{W} \times \mathsf{w})$	$\mathcal{O}(\mathsf{A} \times \mathsf{w})$

Figure 8.1: Comparison of a dictionary and a minimal deterministic automaton

8.1.4 Comparison of the algorithms proposed by Revuz, and Daciuk and Mihov

In section 4.1.3, page 47, we presented an algorithm designed by Dominique Revuz [Revuz, 1992]: after having constructed a deterministic lexicographical tree, we sort it in terms of the heights and we minimize each subset of states having the same height. This algorithm is very fast, since the minimization takes place in time $O(S)$. On the other hand, it requires the construction of a deterministic lexicographic tree, that can use, in the worse case, $O(D)$ space.

On the other hand, the algorithm proposed by Daciuk and Mihov is not as fast ($O(D \times \log(S))$, according to [Mihov, 1999]), but it uses up less space, because its size never exceeds the size of the minimal deterministic automaton $O(S)$ (Figure 8.2).

	Revuz	Daciuk and Mihov
Space used in memory	$O(D)$	$O(S)$
Construction time	$O(S)$	$O(D \times \log(S))$

Figure 8.2: Comparison of the algorithms proposed
by Revuz, and Daciuk and Mihov

8.2 A new structure for the construction

8.2.1 The drawbacks of a representation of a construction using a transition table

Let us have a critical look at the HCLG table in Figure 6.21, page 132, which represents the automaton constructed on the basis of our small dictionary given on page 58. We obtain a table with 22 lines, of which seven are not used. Indeed, when we read the already constructed automaton, every new word adds a new transition, which entails the suppression of one or more lines (which are not removed) and a copy at the end of the table. Moreover, as this happens also in connection with the initial state, we have to store the line corresponding to this state instead of systematically using the first line.

Ideally we would like to store our automaton as a table of states, where the number of transitions to follow varies according to the line.

Let us therefore consider a new data structure:

- We create a column *After*, with the number of transitions after this state. This number, when it was not equal to 1, was given below the cardinal.

- We replace, in our table of states, the columns *Label* and *Goal* with a column *Address* which will indicate where the transitions coming after this state are stored.

- Each state will thus be related to a transition table whose size will be a multiple of the transitions after the state, as in Figure 7.3, where an arrow indicates the address of the transitions.

H	C	A	@	L	G	L	G	L	G

	H	C	A	@	L	G	L	G	L	G
1	6	7	2	→	r	2	s	9		
2	5	6	3	→	a	3	e	6	i	3
3	3	2	2	→	c	4	n	4		
4	2	1	1	→	k	5				
5	1	1	1	→	#	0				
6	4	2	1	→	e	7				
7	3	2	1	→	k	8				
8	2	2	2	→	#	0	s	5		
9	4	1	1	→	e	10				
10	3	1	1	→	e	4				

Figure 8.3: A table of states

8.2.2 A new representation

In order to speed up the look-up of the states that are of interest during minimization, we can also transform this table in a table with linked lists of states, which will allow us to sort them according to certain criteria. The *Goal* is not longer a line number but an address.

For example, the list of states in Figure 8.4 is sorted on the basis of two parameters, the *Height* and the number of transitions after the state.

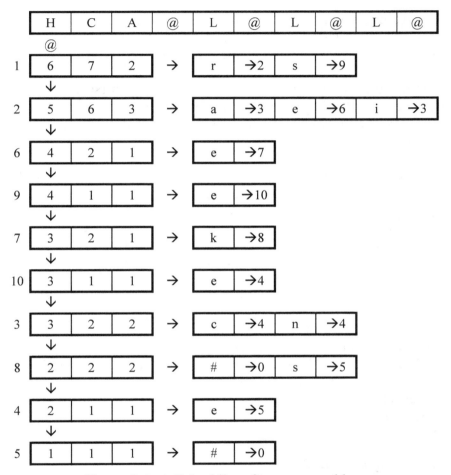

Figure 8.4: A linked list of states sorted by
the heights and the number of following transitions

175

As we can see, this list is rather long. In order to speed up even more the access to the different states that it contains, we can have recourse to a *hash* function, that is, to a direct access to certain elements of the list. The hash table in Figure 8.5 will therefore replace the shaded addresses in Figure 8.4. The first line contains the heights and the second the number of transitions to come, two or more. The last line contains the address of the first state of the sub-list.

	0	1	2	3	4	5	6	7	8	9	10	11	12	13	14	15
H	1		2			3			4			5			6	
A	1	+	2	1	+	2	1	+	2	1	+	2	1	+	2	1
@	5		8	4		3	7			6	2				1	

Figure 8.5: A hash table (height/after)

In order to find the good address list, we multiply the height, reduced by 1, by 3 and we go back 1 if the state has two following transitions or 2 if it has more. Since we use an end-of word character, the words of height 1 only have one following transition, which is labeled with #.

8.2.3 A space gain?

With this new structure, we have suppressed the useless lines and cells, but on the other hand, we have added additional columns. What have we really gained?

In order to compare the two types of representation[58], we will count the number of bytes necessary for each of them. A byte is a popular entity in computer science, and it is based on powers of 2 (see Figure 8.6).

Size	Numerical value	Counts from 0 to
One byte	$2^8 = 256$	255
Two bytes	$(2^8)^2 = 2^{16} = 65\ 536$	65 535
Four bytes	$(2^{16})^2 = 2^{32} = 4\ 294\ 967\ 296$	4 294 967 295

Figure 8.6: The byte as basic element

- The height is maximally the size of the longest word that we suppose to be less than 255 characters (1 byte).

- The largest cardinal is the number of (limited to 4 bytes).

- The label is one character (1 byte).

- The goal is a line number or an address (4 bytes).

---

[58] The comparison of the papers presenting these algorithms is in general quite complex because the implicit data structures are rarely spelled out in detail. One should however consult [Daciuk, 2000] and [Graña *et al.*, 2001].

Figure 8.7 indicates the number of bytes we need to foresee for each element of the transition table.

Height	Cardinal	Label	Goal
1	4	1	4

Total   10

Initial State
4

Total   4

Figure 8.7: Number of bytes necessary for a transition

What about a table of states? We add:

- The address of the transitions (4 bytes).

- The number of following transitions, at most equal to the number of different labels (1 byte).

We then obtain the total number calculated on the basis of Figure 8.8.

Following state	Height	Cardinal	After	Transitions
4	1	4	1	4

Total   14

Label	Goal
1	4

Total   5

Figure 8.8: Number of bytes to reserve for a list of states

Let us now compare the respective size of the two tables for the three examples in Figure 8.9. We will refer to our dictionary on page 111, to the list of French cities and to the *DELAF*[59] dictionary [Courtois, Silberztein, 1990] which contains almost all of the monolexical units of French.

---

[59] We thank Professor Eric Laporte for permission to use this dictionary for research purposes.

	Words	Characters
Example	7	29
Names of French cities	38 198	447 549
General French dictionary	682 418	7 238 120

Figure 8.9: Three dictionaries

Let us calculate the size necessary for the representation of these dictionaries by a transition table; we will carry out these calculations in two ways, first with respect to the total number of lines, and then with respect to the number of lines that are really used (Figure 8.10).

	Lines	Size in Bytes	Lines used	Size in Bytes
Example	22	224	15	154
Cities	48 124	481 244	25 035	250 354
DELAF	870 557	8 705 574	255 194	2 551 944

Figure 8.10: Size of a transition table

Let us now see what is needed in the case of a list of states (Figure 8.11).

	States	Transitions	Size in bytes
Example	10	5	165
Cities	17 859	7 176	285 906
DELAF	139 687	115 507	2 533 153

Figure 8.11: Size of a list of states

When we compare the two tables in Figure 7.11, page 156, and Figure 8.11, we observe that, given the non-used lines, the first structure necessitates more space than the second (Figure 8.12). Of course, we could systematically remove these lines and renumber the table, but this would require significant computing time.

	Improvement (list/table)	
	Lines	Lines used
Example	26%	-7%
Cities	41%	-14%
DELAF	71%	1%

Figure 8.12: Comparison of a table and a list

8.2.4 *What do we really need?*

In the original algorithms of Daciuk and Mihov, there was no mention of height, nor of cardinal, concepts borrowed from Revuz's algorithm. If we remove these two columns, we gain five bytes per state for the table in Figure 8.8, which yields a new size for the list of states (Figure 8.13).

	States	Transitions	Size in bytes
Example	10	5	115
Cities	17 859	7 176	196 611
DELAF	139 687	115 507	1 834 718

Figure 8.13: Size of a list of states
(without heights or cardinals)

If we refrain from calculating *Height*, we can nevertheless make use of a hash table to speed up the look-up of a state in the list (when minimizing). One idea might be to sort the list with respect to the number of the following transitions and with respect to the first transition label as in Figure 8.14.

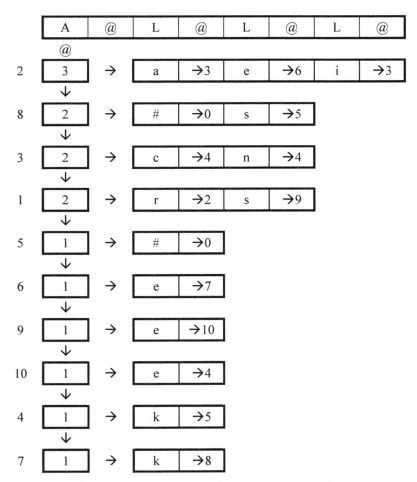

Figure 8.14: A linked list of states sorted
by the number of following transitions and by the first label

The associated hash table is given in Figure 8.15.

A	1			2			3
E	#	e	k	#	c	r	a
@	5	6	4	8	3	1	2

Figure 8.15: A hash table (after/first label)

Recall that the algorithm used by Revuz consists in the creation of a list sorted by *Height*, and without minimization. The *Cardinal* is not needed. When the list is complete, minimization is obtained, *Height-by-Height*. We can obviously take into account the number of following transitions to improve the look-up as in Figure 8.4 and Figure 8.5. The calculation of *Cardinal* allows for the construction of the hash transducer (see section 7.2, page 158).

8.3   A simplified structure for reading

When we construct the automaton (or the transducer) that represents a list of words, we need a lot of information (height, cardinal, number of following transitions, labels, goals.). The HCLG table is designed for the direct and rapid construction of the minimal deterministic automaton. We could store less information, as is proposed by Mihov, who uses only the transitions. This would lead to a reduction of space but entails a loss in speed.

When we use this automaton to analyze a piece of text, we only need the labels and the goals. For this task, we will use the HCLG structure to create a transition table [Daciuk, 2000]. To locate the states, we associate a Boolean to each transition in order to indicate

184

if this transition is the first of the state (1 in the column *Status*) or not (0 in the column *Status*). The table in Figure 8.4 becomes the table SLG in Figure 8.16. Figure 8.17 represents the renumbered automaton.

	Status	Label	Goal
1	1	r	3
2	0	s	14
3	1	a	6
4	0	e	10
5	0	i	6
6	1	c	8
7	0	n	8
8	1	k	9
9	1	#	0
10	1	e	11
11	1	k	12
12	1	#	0
13	0	s	9
14	1	e	15
15	1	e	8

Figure 8.16: The final SLG table

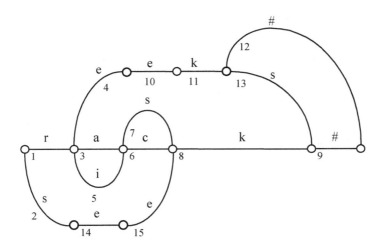

Figure 8.17: The final renumbered automaton

8.4 The output of a transducer

8.4.1 Numbering of the output

Instead of rewriting the same output a number of times, we will put all of them in a table. Let us have look at the final transducer in Figure 7.11, page 156. This transducer yields eight outputs, of which only six are distinct. We put them together in the table[60] in Figure 8.18.

---

[60] This table is sorted lexicographically; upper case V precedes lower case p.

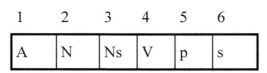

Figure 8.18: A table of outputs

The column *Output* of the transducer (Figure 8.19) will no longer contain a sequence of characters but rather the number of the output in the new table. We use the value *0* to indicate that there is no output.

	Status	Label	Goal	Output
1	1	r	3	0
2	0	s	16	4
3	1	a	6	0
4	0	e	10	2
5	0	i	14	0
6	1	c	8	4
7	0	n	8	1
8	1	k	9	0
9	1	#	0	0
10	1	e	11	0
11	1	k	12	0
12	1	#	0	6
13	0	s	9	5
14	1	c	8	4
15	0	n	8	3
16	1	e	15	0
17	1	e	8	0

Figure 8.19: The SLGO table

The final transducer is thus the one in Figure 8.20.

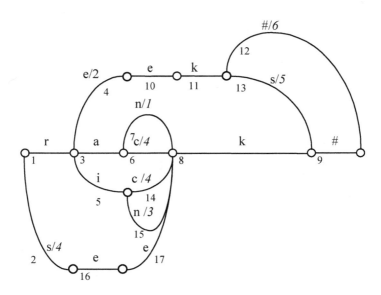

Figure 8.20: The final transducer

8.4.2 Some results

Here are some results concerning the construction of a transducer. We come back to our three dictionaries in Figure 8.9 now in combination with information (Figure 8.21):

- To the French cities, we associate the number of the department (= French political region, 1 to 99).

- To the words in the DELAF dictionary, we associate the lemma (in three different forms[61]) and the morphological code.

The number of outputs obtained is shown Figure 8.22.

---

[61] The first form is complete: the lemma is always present. The second is abbreviated: the lemma is present only if it differs from the word itself. The third is calculated: we indicate the number of letters that need to be removed from the input word to obtain the lemma.

	Entries
Example	rack V
Names of French cities	Tours 37
General dictionary 1	français français.N+z1[62]:ms française français.N+z1:fs
General dictionary 2	français .N+z1:ms française français.N+z1:fs
General dictionary 3	français 0.N+z1:ms française -1.N+z1:fs

Figure 8.21: Five dictionaries

---

[62] The feature $+z1$ encodes that the word *français* is a word of the basic vocabulary. The vocabulary of the DELAF dictionary is divided into three layers [Garrigues, 1993].

	Distinct	Total
Example	6	8
Names of French cities	1 564	35 443
General dictionary 1	258 394	416 211
General dictionary 2	327 260	486 348
General dictionary 3	9 013	81 623

Figure 8.22: The number of outputs for each transducer

The total number of transitions of these transducers is of course different from the total number of transitions of the underlying automata (see section 5.2, page 98), as Figure 8.23 shows.

	Automaton	Transducer
Example	15	18
Names of French cities	25 035	98 026
General dictionary 1		644 656
General dictionary 2	255 194	902 627
General dictionary 3		259 139

Figure 8.23: Comparison of the number of transitions
in the transducer and in the underlying automaton

These examples underscore, clear as it is, the role and importance of the representation of the data. Version 1 of the DELAF dictionary is not well suited. Version 2, which brings about a small reduction compared to the text form (4.8%), is even worse. Only version 3 corresponds to a real compression of the data. The inferior result obtained for the dictionary of French cities is due to a different reason: in contrast to the general language dictionary, the suffixes of these names are too varied to allow significant data compression. The table SLGO of this dictionary takes twice as much space[63] as the text file, whereas the table SLGO of version 3 of the DELAF dictionary takes five times less space.

---

[63] Even though there is no compression here, the access speed is of course a lot better compared to standard dictionary look-up methods.

8.5 An simple application example: tagging text

Consider the following English text:

I seek if you rick your ankle at the rink?
Yes, I do, and it will rack me! it is rank!...

Let us analyze this text with the transducer of Figure 8.20. A first solution (as for instance proposed in linguistic tool boxes like Intex [Silberztein, 1993] or Unitex [Paumier, 2003]), consists in marking the recognized words with braces and in adding the information from the dictionary to the text. In this way we obtain:

I {seek,.V} if you {rick,.V} your ankle at the {rink,.Ns}?
Yes, I do, and it will {rack,.V} me! it is {rank,.A}!...

A more realistic example is given in the following Annex A.

Annex A: A more realistic example

Consider the following paragraph from a biomedical article (extracted completely at random from the Web[64]). We apply two dictionaries to this sample text: a dictionary of polylexical units and a dictionary of monolexical units. We then list the two dictionaries for the text (we only show about one-fourth of the complete text below), and we also mark the polylexical units found in the text portion.

> Bacterial cells have grown in the biofilm phenotype for billions of years, as part of their successful strategy to colonize most of this planet and its life forms. Microbiologists have only recognized this distinct phenotype as the predominant mode of bacterial growth for the last two decades. While being an important survival mechanism for the bacteria, it represents a double-edged sword for their habitats and surroundings. Microbial biofilms are involved in approximately 65% of human bacterial infections, and up to 60% of hospital acquired infections are caused by biofilms that contaminate implants and catheters. Microbial biofilms are also implicated in human infections such as otitis media, necrotizing fasciitis, osteomyelitis, bacterial prostatitis, infective endocarditis, cystic fibrosis pneumonia, and oral diseases such as dental caries and periodontal disease. The biofilms involved consist of microorganisms enveloped in extracellular polymeric substances, organized in threedimensional structures, with networks of intervening water channels and multiple layers of cells. A modern definition of a biofilm must take into consideration these readily observable characteristics, but also embrace other physiological attributes, including altered growth rate and the fact that biofilm organisms transcribe genes that planktonic organisms do not. The structural and the physiological attributes of biofilm organisms confer an inherent resistance to, for example, host defences,

---

[64] The entire text contains 2700 lexical units of which 928 are different.

antibiotics, antiseptics and shear forces. While antibiotic therapy typically reverses the symptoms caused by bacteria in suspension, it often fails to kill the biofilm microorganisms. For this reason, biofilm infections often show recurrent symptoms after antibiotic therapy. Decreased bacterial growth rate, decreased diffusion into the biofilm, biofilm specific substances such as exopolysaccharides and the differential gene expression are possible reasons for the resistance of biofilms. The differential gene expression pattern during biofilm formation may involve intercellular signalling. Factors involved in the transition from a free-floating, planktonic existence to that of a surface-attached, sessile community are complex. Given the widespread distribution of infections caused by biofilms and its resistance to antimicrobials, a better understanding of the bacterial interactions influencing biofilm formation and biofilms is of high importance. One bacterial inter-cellular communication mechanism, which might influence biofilm formation, is dependent of the so-called competence genes. The change in gene expression profile in response to becoming a member of a biofilm community seems to involve, at least in part, surface-sensing mechanisms, which are dependent on, cell density. The "language" used for this inter-cellular communication is based on small, self-generated signal molecules termed quorum-sensing signals. Quorum sensing has been found to regulate a number of physiological activities, including induction of genetic competence in oral streptococci. Competence for genetic transformation is a physiological state that allows binding, processing and integration of exogenous DNA.

We found 96 polylexical units in the entire text and yet 64 in the text portion.

List of polylexical units found in the text:

antibiotic therapy,.N:s
at least,.ADV
bacterial cells,bacterial cell.N:p
bacterial growth,.N:s
bacterial growth rate,.N:s

bacterial interactions,bacterial interaction.N:p
bacterial inter-cellular communication mechanism,. N:s
bacterial prostatitis,.N:s

biofilm community,.N:s
biofilm formation,.N:s
biofilm infections,.N:p
biofilm microorganisms,biofilm
microorganism.N:p
biofilm organisms, biofilm
organism.N:p
biofilm phenotype,.N:s
cell density,.N:s
competence genes,.competence
gene.N:p
cystic fibrosis pneumonia, N:s
dental caries,dental carie.N:p
double-edged sword,.N:s
exogenous DNA,.N:s
extracellular polymeric
substances,extracellular polymeric
substance.N:p
free-floating,.A
gene expression,.N:s
gene expression pattern,.N:s
gene expression profile,.N:s
genetic competence,.N:s
genetic transformation,.N:s
growth rate,.N:s
high importance,.N:s
hospital acquired infections,hospital
acquired infection.N:p
host defences, host defence.N:p
human bacterial infections,human
bacterial infection.N:p
human infections,human
infection.N:p
in part,.ADV
infective endocarditis,.N:s
inherent resistance,.N:s
inter-cellular communication,.N:s

intercellular signalling,.N:s
microbial biofilms, microbial
biofilm.N:p
modern definition,.N:s
multiple layers,multiple layer.N:p
necrotizing fasciitis,.N:s
observable characteristics,
observable characteristic.N:p
oral diseases,oral disease.N:p
oral streptococci,oral
streptococcus.N:p
otitis media,.N:s
periodontal disease,.N:s
physiological activities,
physiological activity.N:p
physiological
attributes,physiological
attribute.N:p
physiological state,.N:s
planktonic existence,.N:s
planktonic organisms,planktonic
organism.N:p
predominant mode,.N:s
quorum sensing,.N:s
quorum-sensing signals, quorum-
sensing signal.N:p
sessile community,.N:s
signal molecules,signal
molecule.N:p
so-called,.A
successful strategy,.N:s
surface-attached,.A
surface-sensing
mechanisms,surface-sensing
mechanism.N:p
survival mechanism,.N:s
water channels,water channel.N:p

widespread distribution,.N:s

Recognition of polylexical units in the sample text portion:

<Bacterial cells> have grown in the <biofilm phenotype> for billions of years, as part of their <successful strategy> to colonize most of this planet and its <life forms>. Microbiologists have only recognized this distinct phenotype as the <predominant mode> of <bacterial growth> for the last two decades. While being an important <survival mechanism> for the bacteria, it represents a <double-edged sword> for their habitats and surroundings. <Microbial biofilms> are involved in approximately 65% of <human bacterial infections>, and up to 60% of <hospital acquired infections> are caused by biofilms that contaminate implants and catheters. <Microbial biofilms> are also implicated in <human infections> such as <otitis media>, <necrotizing fasciitis>, osteomyelitis, <bacterial prostatitis>, <infective endocarditis>, <cystic fibrosis pneumonia>, and <oral diseases> such as <dental caries> and <periodontal disease>. The biofilms involved consist of microorganisms enveloped in <extracellular polymeric substances>, organized in threedimensional structures, with networks of intervening <water channels> and <multiple layers> of cells. A <modern definition> of a biofilm must take into consideration these readily <observable characteristics>, but also embrace other <physiological attributes>, including altered <growth rate> and the fact that <biofilm organisms> transcribe genes that <planktonic organisms> do not. The structural and the <physiological attributes> of <biofilm organisms> confer an <inherent resistance> to, for example, <host defences>, antibiotics, antiseptics and shear forces. While <antibiotic therapy> typically reverses the symptoms caused by bacteria in suspension, it often fails to kill the <biofilm microorganisms>. For this reason, <biofilm infections> often show recurrent symptoms after <antibiotic therapy>. Decreased <bacterial growth rate>, decreased diffusion into the biofilm, biofilm specific substances such as exopolysaccharides and the differential <gene expression> are possible reasons for the resistance of biofilms. The differential <gene expression pattern> during <biofilm formation> may involve <intercellular signalling>. Factors involved in the transition from

a <free-floating>, <planktonic existence> to that of a <surface-attached>, <sessile community> are complex. Given the <widespread distribution> of infections caused by biofilms and its resistance to antimicrobials, a better understanding of the <bacterial interactions> influencing <biofilm formation> and biofilms is of <high importance>. One <bacterial inter-cellular communication mechanism>, which might influence <biofilm formation>, is dependent of the <so-called> <competence genes>. The change in <gene expression profile> in response to becoming a member of a <biofilm community> seems to involve, <at least> <in part>, <surface-sensing mechanisms> which are dependent on <cell density>. The "language" used for this <inter-cellular communication> is based on small, self-generated <signal molecules> termed <quorum-sensing signals>. <Quorum sensing> has been found to regulate a number of <physiological activities>, including induction of <genetic competence> in <oral streptococci>. Competence for <genetic transformation> is a <physiological state> that allows binding, processing and integration of <exogenous DNA>.

The above annotation is based purely on lexical look-up in a large dictionary of polylexical units in English (of more than 1 million items). This look-up shows among other things that the percentage of forms that need to be recognized as multi-word items is relatively high in text (somewhere between 20 and 30 % on the average) and this is of course a lower bound given that there are still very many multi-word lexical items that result of grammatical transducers still to be identified. On the other hand, such experiments show that it is indeed possible to construct very precise and large-scale dictionaries for a given language. Without such precise and fast identification of the lexical units in arbitrary text, all further operations (from statistical word counting to symbolic ones like parsing) will be prone to a high degree of error.

We found 1351 monolexical units in the entire text and 399 in the text portion.

List of monolexical units found in the text portion:

a,.DET:s
a,.N:s
acquired,.A
acquired,acquire.V:K:I1s:I2s:I3s:I1p:I2p:I3p
activities,activity.N:p
after,.A
after,.ADV
after,.CONJ
after,.PREP
allows,allow.V:P3s
also,.ADV
altered,alter.V:K:I1s:I2s:I3s:I1p:I2p:I3p
an,a.DET:s
and,.CONJ
and,.V:W:P1s:P2s:P1p:P2p:P3p
antibiotic,.A
antibiotic,.N:s
antibiotics,antibiotic.N:p
antimicrobials,antimicrobial.N:p
antiseptics,antiseptic.N:p
approximately,.ADV
are,.N:s
are,be.V:P2s:P1p:P2p:P3p
as,.ADV
as,.CONJ
as,.N:s:p
as,.PREP
as,a.N:p
at,.PREP
attached,.A
attached,attach.V:K:I1s:I2s:I3s:I1p:I2p:I3p
attributes,attribute.N:p
202

attributes,attribute.V:P3s
bacteria,bacterium.N:p
bacterial,.A
based,.A
based,base.V:K:I1s:I2s:I3s:I1p:I2p:I3p
becoming,.A
becoming,.N:s
becoming,become.V:G
been,.N:s
been,be.V:K
being,.A
being,.N:s
being,.N:s
being,be.V:G
better,.ADV
better,.N:s
better,.V:W:P1s:P2s:P1p:P2p:P3p
better,good.A:C
billions,.DET:p
billions,billion.N:p
binding,.A
binding,.N:s
binding,bind.V:G
but,.ADV
but,.CONJ
but,.PREP
by,.PART
by,.PREP
called,call.V:K:I1s:I2s:I3s:I1p:I2p:I3p
caries,.N:s:p
catheters,catheter.N:p
caused,cause.V:K:I1s:I2s:I3s:I1p:I2p:I3p

cell,.N:s
cells,cell.N:p
cellular,.A
change,.N:s
change,.V:W:P1s:P2s:P1p:P2p:P3p
channels,channel.N:p
channels,channel.V:P3s
characteristics,characteristic.N:p
colonize,.V:W:P1s:P2s:P1p:P2p:P3p
communication,.N:s
community,.N:s
competence,.N:s
complex,.A
complex,.N:s
confer,.V:W:P1s:P2s:P1p:P2p:P3p
consideration,.N:s
consist,.V:W:P1s:P2s:P1p:P2p:P3p
contaminate,.V:W:P1s:P2s:P1p:P2p:P3p
cystic,.A
decades,decade.N:p
decreased,decrease.V:K:I1s:I2s:I3s:I1p:I2p:I3p
defences,defence.N:p
definition,.N:s
density,.N:s
dental,.A
dental,.N:s
dependent,.A
dependent,.N:s
differential,.A
differential,.N:s
diffusion,.N:s
disease,.N:s
diseases,disease.N:p
distinct,.A

distribution,.N:s
DNA,.N:s:p
do,.N:s
do,.V:W:P1s:P2s:P1p:P2p:P3p
double,.A
double,.ADV
double,.N:s
double,.V:W:P1s:P2s:P1p:P2p:P3p
during,.PREP
edged,.A
edged,edge.V:K:I1s:I2s:I3s:I1p:I2p:I3p
embrace,.N:s
embrace,.V:W:P1s:P2s:P1p:P2p:P3p
endocarditis,.N:s
enveloped,.A
enveloped,envelop.V:K:I1s:I2s:I3s:I1p:I2p:I3p
example,.N:s
example,.V:W:P1s:P2s:P1p:P2p:P3p
existence,.N:s
exogenous,.A
expression,.N:s
extracellular,.A
fact,.N:s
factors,factor.N:p
factors,factor.N:p
factors,factor.V:P3s
fails,fail.N:p
fails,fail.V:P3s
fasciitis,.N:s
fibrosis,.N:s
floating,.A
floating,.N:s
floating,float.V:G

for,.CONJ
for,.PREP
forces,force.N:p
forces,force.V:P3s
formation,.N:s
forms,form.N:p
forms,form.V:P3s
found,.N:s
found,.V:W:P1s:P2s:P1p:P2p:P3p
found,find.V:K:I1s:I2s:I3s:I1p:I2p:
I3p
free,.A
free,.ADV
free,.V:W:P1s:P2s:P1p:P2p:P3p
from,.PREP
gene,.N:s
generated,generate.V:K:I1s:I2s:I3s:
I1p:I2p:I3p
genes,gene.N:p
genetic,.A
given,.A
given,.N:s
given,give.V:K
grown,.A
grown,grow.V:K
growth,.N:s
habitats,habitat.N:p
has,have.V:P3s
have,.N:s
have,.V:W:P1s:P2s:P1p:P2p:P3p
high,.A
high,.ADV
high,.N:s
hospital,.N:s
host,.N:s
host,.N:s
host,.N:s

host,.V:W:P1s:P2s:P1p:P2p:P3p
human,.A
human,.N:s
implants,implant.N:p
implants,implant.V:P3s
implicated,implicate.V:K:I1s:I2s:I3
s:I1p:I2p:I3p
importance,.N:s
important,.A
in,.A
in,.N:s
in,.PART
in,.PREP
including,include.V:G
induction,.N:s
infections,infection.N:p
infective,.A
influence,.N:s
influence,.V:W:P1s:P2s:P1p:P2p:P
3p
influencing,influence.V:G
inherent,.A
integration,.N:s
inter,.N:s
inter,.PFX
inter,.V:W:P1s:P2s:P1p:P2p:P3p
interactions,interaction.N:p
intercellular,.A
intervening,.A
intervening,.N:s
intervening,intervene.V:G
into,.PART
into,.PREP
involve,.V:W:P1s:P2s:P1p:P2p:P3p
involved,.A
involved,involve.V:K:I1s:I2s:I3s:I1
p:I2p:I3p

is,be.V:P3s
is,i.N:p
it,.PRO:3ns
its,.DET:s:p
its,.PRO:s:p
kill,.N:s
kill,.V:W:P1s:P2s:P1p:P2p:P3p
language,.N:s
last,.A
last,.ADV
last,.N:s
last,.V:W:P1s:P2s:P1p:P2p:P3p
layers,layer.N:p
layers,layer.N:p
layers,layer.V:P3s
least,.A:S
least,.ADV
life,.N:s
may,.N:s
may,.N:s
may,.V:W:P1s:P2s:P3s:P1p:P2p:P3p
mechanism,.N:s
mechanisms,mechanism.N:p
media,.N:s
media,medium.N:p
member,.N:s
member,.N:s
member,.N:s
microbial,.A
microbiologists,microbiologist.N:p
microorganisms,microorganism.N:p
might,.N:s
might,may.V:I1s:I2s:I3s:I1p:I2p:I3p
mode,.N:s
modern,.A

modern,.N:s
molecules,molecule.N:p
most,.ADV
most,.DET:s:p
most,.PRO:s:p
multiple,.A
multiple,.N:s
must,.N:s
must,.V:P1s:P2s:P3s:P1p:P2p:P3p
necrotizing,necrotize.V:G
networks,network.N:p
networks,network.V:P3s
not,.ADV
number,.N:s
number,.V:W:P1s:P2s:P1p:P2p:P3p
number,numb.A:C
observable,.A
observable,.N:s
of,.PREP
often,.ADV
on,.A
on,.PART
on,.PREP
one,.DET:s
one,.N:s
one,.PRO:3s
only,.A
only,.ADV
only,.CONJ
only,.PRED
oral,.A
oral,.N:s
organisms,organism.N:p
organized,organize.V:K:I1s:I2s:I3s:I1p:I2p:I3p
osteomyelitis,.N:s
other,.ADV

other,.DET
otitis,.N:s
part,.ADV
part,.N:s
part,.V:W:P1s:P2s:P1p:P2p:P3p
pattern,.N:s
pattern,.V:W:P1s:P2s:P1p:P2p:P3p
periodontal,.A
phenotype,.N:s
physiological,.A
planet,.N:s
planktonic,.A
pneumonia,.N:s
polymeric,.A
possible,.A
possible,.N:s
predominant,.A
processing,.N:s
processing,process.V:G
profile,.N:s
profile,.V:W:P1s:P2s:P1p:P2p:P3p
prostatitis,.N:s
quorum,.N:s
rate,.N:s
rate,.V:W:P1s:P2s:P1p:P2p:P3p
readily,.ADV
reason,.N:s
reason,.V:W:P1s:P2s:P1p:P2p:P3p
reasons,reason.N:p
reasons,reason.V:P3s
recognized,recognize.V:K:I1s:I2s:I
3s:I1p:I2p:I3p
recurrent,.A
regulate,.V:W:P1s:P2s:P1p:P2p:P3
p
represents,represent.V:P3s
resistance,.N:s

response,.N:s
reverses,reverse.N:p
reverses,reverse.V:P3s
seems,seem.V:P3s
self,.N:s
self,.PFX
sensing,.N:s
sensing,sense.V:G
sessile,.A
shear,.N:s
shear,.V:W:P1s:P2s:P1p:P2p:P3p
show,.N:s
show,.V:W:P1s:P2s:P1p:P2p:P3p
signal,.A
signal,.N:s
signal,.V:W:P1s:P2s:P1p:P2p:P3p
signalling,.N:s
signalling,signal.V:G
signals,signal.N:p
signals,signal.V:P3s
small,.A
small,.ADV
so,.ADV
so,.CONJ
specific,.A
specific,.N:s
state,.N:s
state,.V:W:P1s:P2s:P1p:P2p:P3p
strategy,.N:s
streptococci,streptococcus.N:p
structural,.A
structural,.N:s
structures,structure.N:p
structures,structure.V:P3s
substances,substance.N:p
successful,.A
such,.DET:s:p

such,.PRED
such,.PRO:s:p
surface,.N:s
surface,.V:W:P1s:P2s:P1p:P2p:P3p
surroundings,.N:p
surroundings,surrounding.N:p
survival,.N:s
survival,.N:s
suspension,.N:s
sword,.N:s
symptoms,symptom.N:p
take,.N:s
take,.V:W:P1s:P2s:P1p:P2p:P3p
termed,term.V:K:I1s:I2s:I3s:I1p:I2
p:I3p
that,.ADV
that,.CONJ
that,.DET:s
that,.PRO:s
the,.DET:s:p
their,.DET:s:p
therapy,.N:s
these,.DET:p
these,.PRO:p
this,.ADV
this,.DET:s
this,.PRO:s
threedimensional,.A
to,.PART
to,.PREP

transcribe,.V:W:P1s:P2s:P1p:P2p:P
3p
transformation,.N:s
transition,.N:s
two,.DET:p
two,.N:s
typically,.ADV
understanding,.A
understanding,.N:s
understanding,understand.V:G
up,.A
up,.N:s
up,.PART
up,.PREP
up,.V:W:P1s:P2s:P1p:P2p:P3p
used,.A
used,use.V:K:I1s:I2s:I3s:I1p:I2p:I3
p
water,.N:s
water,.V:W:P1s:P2s:P1p:P2p:P3p
which,.DET:s:p
which,.DET:s:p
which,.PRO:s:p
while,.CONJ
while,.N:s
while,.V:W:P1s:P2s:P1p:P2p:P3p
widespread,.A
with,.PREP
years,year.N:p

As inspection of the above text and lists shows, the "off-the-shelf" coverage of the dictionaries we used is extremely high and precise; this is not very surprising because both the general English dictionaries for monolexical and polylexical units have been curated over more than ten years now.

In addition to a handful of proper names, abbreviations and acronyms, respectively, the lexical look-up also revealed almost a dozen orthographic errors as well as a couple of incorrect lexical annotations, due to the ad-hoc use of the words in question. Clearly thus use of acronyms and abbreviations requires a special component to identify the intended uses of these forms. This is related to the general issue of how to resolve the large number of ambiguities that result from lexical look-up; we have not addressed this issue at all in this book since it is not directly related to matters of dictionary construction and implementation. It is indeed interesting to note that almost every word in the sample text has at least two if not more distinct morphosyntactic interpretations attached to it and these need to be separated out for any further linguistic processing (e.g. information extraction, parsing, translation, etc.).

There are of course many approaches to this problem in the computational linguistic literature ranging from purely statistical and purely analytical to mixed approaches drawing upon both of the former in various ways. There are many other issues related to the construction and the use of such dictionaries, e.g. the problems related to the treatment of orthographic variants (for instance, hyphenated and non-hyphenated variants), of rare interpretations of words (e.g. the analysis of (alphabetic) letters as nouns in the dictionaries above), spurious categorizations of "grammatical words", and many other topics that need to be addressed if one wants to achieve an ideal coverage of the lexical material of a given natural language.

208

Annex B: Solution to exercises

Number 1, page 91

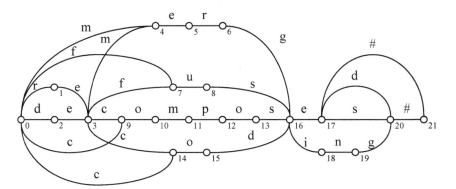

The resulting automaton

Number 2, page 91

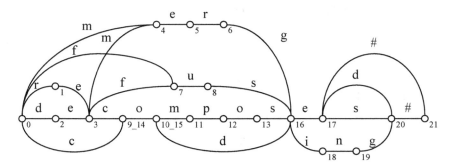

The deterministic automaton

Number 1, page 105

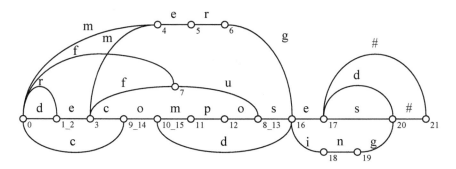

The minimal deterministic automaton

Number 2, page 105

$\mathbf{z}_0 = \{21\}$ $\mathbf{z}_1 = \{20\}$ $\mathbf{z}_2 = \{17, 19\}$ $\mathbf{z}_3 = \{18\}$

$\mathbf{z}_4 = \{16\}$ $\mathbf{z}_5 = \{6, 8, 13\}$ $\mathbf{z}_6 = \{5, 7, 12\}$ $\mathbf{z}_7 = \{4, 11\}$

$\mathbf{z}_8 = \{10\_15\}$ $\mathbf{z}_9 = \{9\_14\}$ $\mathbf{z}_{10} = \{3\}$ $\mathbf{z}_{11} = \{1, 2\}$

$\mathbf{z}_{12} = \{0\}$

The height classes

The minimization occurs in $\mathbf{z}_5$ and $\mathbf{z}_{11}$.

Number 3, page 105

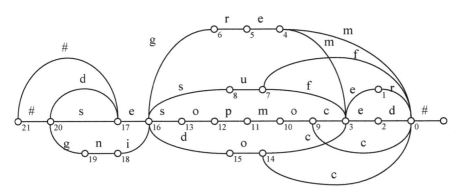

The reverse automaton

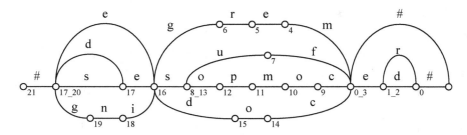

The deterministic reverse automaton

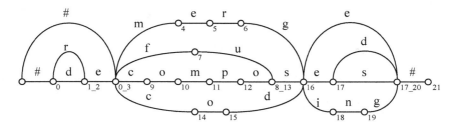

The reverse automaton of the deterministic reverse automaton

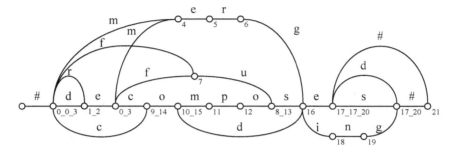

The minimal deterministic automaton

Number 1, page 145

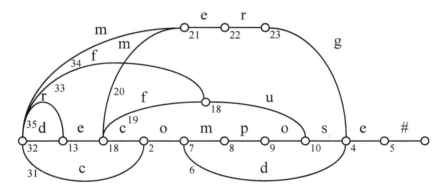

The minimal deterministic automaton

Number 2, page 145

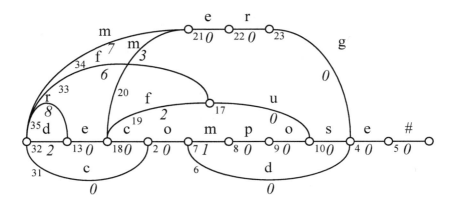

The minimal deterministic automaton

Page 166

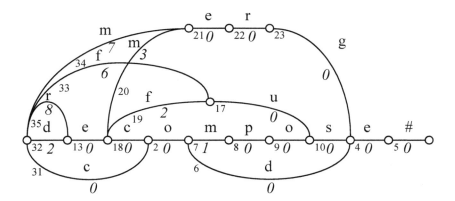

The hash transducer

References

Abney S. (1996), Partial parsing via finite-state cascades, *J. of Natural Language Engineering*, 2-4: 337-344.

Béal M-P., Carton O. (2001), Computing the prefix of an automaton, *RAIRO Theoret. Comput. Sci.*, 34-6:503-515.

Beesley K., Kartunnen L. (2003), *Finite-state Morphology*, CSLI Studies in Computational Linguistics, CSLI Publications.

Berstel J., Carton O. (2004), On the complexity of Hopcroft's state minimization algorithm, *CIAA 2004*, LNCS 3317, 35-44.

Blanco X. (1997), Noms composés et traduction français-espagnol, *Lingvisticae Investigationes*, XXI-2:321-348.

Brzozowski J. A. (1962a), Canonical regular expressions and minimal state graphs for definite events, *Mathematical Theory of Automata*, MRI Symposia Series, 12:529-561.

Brzozowski J. A. (1962b), *Regular expression techniques for sequential circuits*, Ph.D. dissertation, Princeton University, Princeton, New Jersey.

217

Carrasco R. C., Forcada M. L. (2002), Incremental construction and maintenance of minimal finite-state automata, Computational Linguistics, 28-2:207-216.

Chinchor N. (1997), *Muc-7 Named Entity Task Definition*, http://www.itl.nist.gov/iaui/894.02/related_projects/muc/proceedin gs/muc_7_toc.html#appendices.

Choffrut C. (2003), Minimizing subsequential transducers: a survey, *TCS* 292-1:131-143.

Ciura M., Deorowicz S. (1999), *Experimental study of finite automata storing static lexicons*, Technical Report BW-453/RAu-2/99, Silesian Technical University, Poland.

Coates-Stephens S. (1993), *The Analysis and Acquisition of Proper Names for the Understanding of Free Text*, Kluwer Academic Publishers, Hingham, MA.

Courtois B., Silberztein M. (1990), Dictionnaires électroniques du français, *Langues française*, 87:11-22.

Crochemore M., Vérin R. (1997), On compact Directed Acyclic Word Graphs, *LNCS* 1261, 192-211.

Daciuk J., (1998), *Incremental Construction of Finite-State Automata and Transducers, and their Use in the Natural Language Processing*, Ph.D. dissertation, Technical University of Gdańsk, Poland.

Daciuk J. (2000), Experiments with Automata Compression, *CIAA 2000*, LNCS 2088:105-112.

218

Daciuk J., Mihov S., Watson B. W., Watson R. E. (2000), Incremental construction of Minimal Acyclic Finite-state Automata, *Computational Linguistics*, 26-1:3-16.

Daciuk J., Watson B. W., Watson R. E. (1998), Incremental construction of Minimal Acyclic Finite-state Automata and Transducers, Proceedings of *FSMNLP*, 48-56.

Engelke S. (2003), *Freie und feste Adverbiale im Deutschen*, CIS, University of Munich.

Friburger N. (2002), *Reconnaissance automatique des noms propres ; application à la classification automatique de textes journalistiques*, thèse de doctorat en informatique, Université de Tours.

Friburger N., Maurel D. (2004), Finite-state transducer cascades to extract named entities in texts, *Theoretical Computer Science*, 313:94-104.

Garrigues M. (1993), *Méthode de paramétrage des dictionnaires et grammaires électroniques: Application à des systèmes interactifs en langue naturelle*, thèse de doctorat en Sciences du language, Université Paris 7.

Graña J., Barcala F-M., Alonso M. A. (2001), Compilation methods of minimal acyclic finite-state automata for large dictionaries, Proceedings of *CIAA 2001*, 135-148.

Gross G., Guenthner F. (to appear), *Manuel de lexicographie*.

Gross M. (1975), *Méthodes en syntaxe*, Hermann, Paris.

219

Gross M. (1986), Lexicon-grammar. The Representation of Compound Words, COLING 1986, 1-6.

Gross M. (1989), The use of finite automata in the lexical representation of natural language, *LNCS* 377:34-50.

Gross M. (1990), *Grammaire transformationnelle du français : syntaxe de l'adverbe*, ASSTRIL, Paris.

Gross M. (1999), Lemmatization of compound tenses in English, *Lingvisticae Investigationes*, XXII:71-122.

Gross M., Perrin D. (1989), editors, *Electronic Dictionaries and Automata in Computational Linguistics*, LNCS 377.

Gross M., Senellart J. (1998), Nouvelles bases statistiques pour les mots du français, *JADT 98*, 335-350

Guenthner F. (2002), A remark about the size of electronic dictionaries, *Bulag*, 33-41.

Guenthner F. (to appear), *Corpus Calculus in a Nutshell*, CIS, University of Munich.

Guenthner F., Meier P. (1995), Das CISLEX-Wörterbuchsystem, Lexikagraphica.

Guenthner F., Blanco X. (2004), Multi-lexemic expressions: an overview, *Lingvisticae Investigationes Suplementa*, 24:239-252.

Halpern J. (2000), Is English Segmentation Trivial?, http://www.cjk.org/cjk/reference/engmorph.htm.

Holzmann G. J., Puri A. (1999), A minimized automaton representation of reachable states, *International Journal on Software Tools for Technology Transfer*, 2-4:270-278.

Hopcroft J. (1971), An *n* log *n* algorithm for minimizing states in a finite automaton, *International Symposium on Theory of Machines and Computations.*, Haifa, Israel, 189-196.

Hopcroft J., Ullman J. (1979), *Introduction to Automata Theory, Languages and Computation*, Reading, Mass., Addison-Wesley.

Lucchesi C. L., Kowaltowski T. (1993), Applications of Finite Automata Representing Large Vocabularies, *Softw., Pract. Exper.*, 23-1:15-30.

Krstev S., Vitas D., Maurel D., Tran M. (2005), Multilingual ontology of proper names, Second Language & Technology Conference, 116-119.

Labonté A. (1998), *Technique de réduction - Tris informatiques à quatre clés*, Government of Québec, url on the web: http://www.lirmm.fr/~lafourca/Souk/trif/techniques-de-tri.html.

Laporte E. (1988), *Méthodes algorithmiques et lexicales de phonétisation de textes : applications au français*, thèse de doctorat en informatique, Université Paris 7.

Liang F. M. (1983), *Word hyphenation by computer*, PhD Thesis, Computer Science Departement, Standford University, Research Report STAN-CS-83-977.

Maier-Meyer P. (1995), *Lexikon und automatische Lemmatisierung*, , CIS-Bericht-95-84, University of Munich.

Mathieu-Colas M. (1988), Variations graphiques des mots composés dans le Petit Larousse et le Petit Robert. *Lingvisticae Investigationes*, 12-2:235-280.

Maurel D. (1989), *Reconnaissance de séquences de mots par automate, adverbes de date du Français*, thèse de doctorat en informatique, Université Paris 7.

Maurel D. (1996), Building automaton on Schemata and Acceptability Tables, *WIA '96*, in *LNCS*, 1260:72-86.

Mel'cuk I. (1988), Paraphrase et lexique dans la théorie linguistique Sens-Texte, *Lexique* 6:13-54.

Mel'cuk I. (1998), The meaning-text approach to the study of natural language and linguistic functional models, *LACUS Forum* 24, 3-20.

Mihov S. (1998), On-line algorithm for building minimal automaton Presenting Finite Language, *Annuaire de l'Université de Sofia St. Kl. Ohridski*, Faculté de Mathématiques et Informatique, volume 91, livre 1.

Mihov S. (1999), Direct construction of minimal acyclic finite states automata, *Annuaire de l'Université de Sofia St. Kl. Ohridski*, Faculté de Mathématiques et Informatique, volume 92, livre 2.

Mihov S., Maurel D. (2000), Direct construction of minimal acyclic sub- sequential transducers, *CIAA'2000*, LNCS 2088:217-229.

Mohri M. (1994), Minimization of sequential transducers, *CPM'94*, LNCS 807:151-163.

Mohri M. (1996), On some applications of finite-state automata theory to natural language processing, *Natural Language Engineering*, 2:1-20.

Mohri M. (1997), Finite-state transducers in language and speech processing, *Computational Linguistics*, 23-2:269-311.

Mohri M. (2000), Minimization Algorithms for Sequential Transducers, *Theoretical Computer Science*, 234:177-201.

Moore E. F. (1956), Gedanken expriments on sequential machines, *Automata Studies*, 129-156.

Myhill J. (1957), Finite automata and representation of events, *Fund Concepts in the Theory of Systems*, 57-624.

Paik W., Liddy E. D., Yu E., McKenna M. (1996), Categorizing and standardizing proper nouns for efficient information retrieval, *Corpus Processing for Lexical Acquisition*, 61-73, Massachussetts Institute of Technology.

Paumier S. (2003), *De la reconnaissance de formes linguistiques à l'analyse syntaxique*, thèse de doctorat en informatique, Université de Marne-la-Vallée.

Paumier S. (2004), Recursive automata for syntactic grammars, *Lexicon-Grammar Workshop*, Beijing, 16-17 oct; 2004.

Perrin D. (1995), Les débuts de la théorie des automatons, *Technique et Science Informatique*, 14:409-443.

Ranchod E., Mota ., Baptista J. (1999), A computational lexicon of Portuguese for automatic text parsing, SIGLEX-99.

Revuz D. (1991), *Dictionnaires et lexiques - Méthodes et algorithmes*, thèse de doctorat en informatique, Université Paris 7.

Revuz D. (1992), Minimization of acyclic deterministic automata in linear time, *Theoretical Computer Science*, 92:181-189.

Revuz D. (2000), Dynamic acyclic minimal automaton, *CIAA 2000*, LNCS 2088:226-232.

Roche E., Schabes Y. (1997), editors, *Finite-state Language Processing*, Cambridge, Mass./London, England: MIT Press.

Roche E. (1993), *Analyse syntaxique transformationnelle de français par transducteurs et lexique-grammaires*, thèse de doctorat en Informatique, Université Paris 7.

Roche E. (1999), Finite-state transducers: parsing free and frozen sentences, *Studies in natural language processing*, 108-120.

Salkoff M. (1992), On using the French lexicon-grammar in a French-English bilingual dictionary, *Papers in Computational Lexicography*'92, Kiefer F, Kiss G. et Pajzs J. (eds), Linguistics Institute Hungarian Academy of Sciences, Budapest.

224

Savary A. (2000), *Recensement et description des mots composés – méthodes et applications*, thèse de doctorat en informatique, Université Paris 7.

Savary A. (2005), Towards a formalism for the computational morphology of multi-word units, Second *Language & Technology Conference*, 305-309.

Senellart J. (1998), Locating noun phrases with finite-state transducers, COLING-ACL 1998, 1212-1219.

Senellart J. (1999), *Outils de reconnaissance d'expressions linguistiques complexes dans des grands corpus*, thèse de doctorat en informatique, Université Paris 7.

Silberztein M. (1993), *Dictionnaires électroniques et analyse automatique de textes - Le système INTEX*, Paris, Masson.

Tran M., Maurel D., Savary A. (2005), Implantation d'un tri lexical respectant la particularité des noms propres, *Lingvisticae Investigationes*, XXVIII-2 (to appear).

Watson B. W. (1995), *Taxonomies and Toolkits of Regular Language Algorithms*, Thesis Technische Universiteit Eindhoven.

Watson B. W. (1998), A fast new semi-incremental algorithm for the Construction of Minimal Acyclic DFAs, *WIA'98*, LNCS 1660:121-132.

Watson B. W. (2001), A taxonomy of algorithms for constructing minimal acyclic deterministic finite automata, *South African Comput. J.*, 27:12-17.

Watson B. W. (2003), A new algorithm for the construction of minimal acyclic DFAs, *Science of Computer Programming*, 48-2-3:81-97.

Table of figures

Table of index

Roche, 9, 44, 45

Salkoff, 26

Salyzniak, 34

Savary, 22, 39

Schabes, 9

Senellart, 22, 44

Silberztein, 35, 42, 181, 197

SLG, 187

SLGO, 192

state

    convergent, 107, 118, 139

    divergent, 107

    final, 49, 66, 73, 96

    initial, 49, 65, 73, 74

terminal, 70

Tran, 39

transducer, 57, 76

    hash, 164

    sub-sequential, 74

transition, 49, 65, 73, 74

    ε-transition, 69, 70, 71, 72, 81, 83

transition table, 79

Ullman, 83, 96

Vitas, 39

Watson, 55, 83, 109

Yu, 39